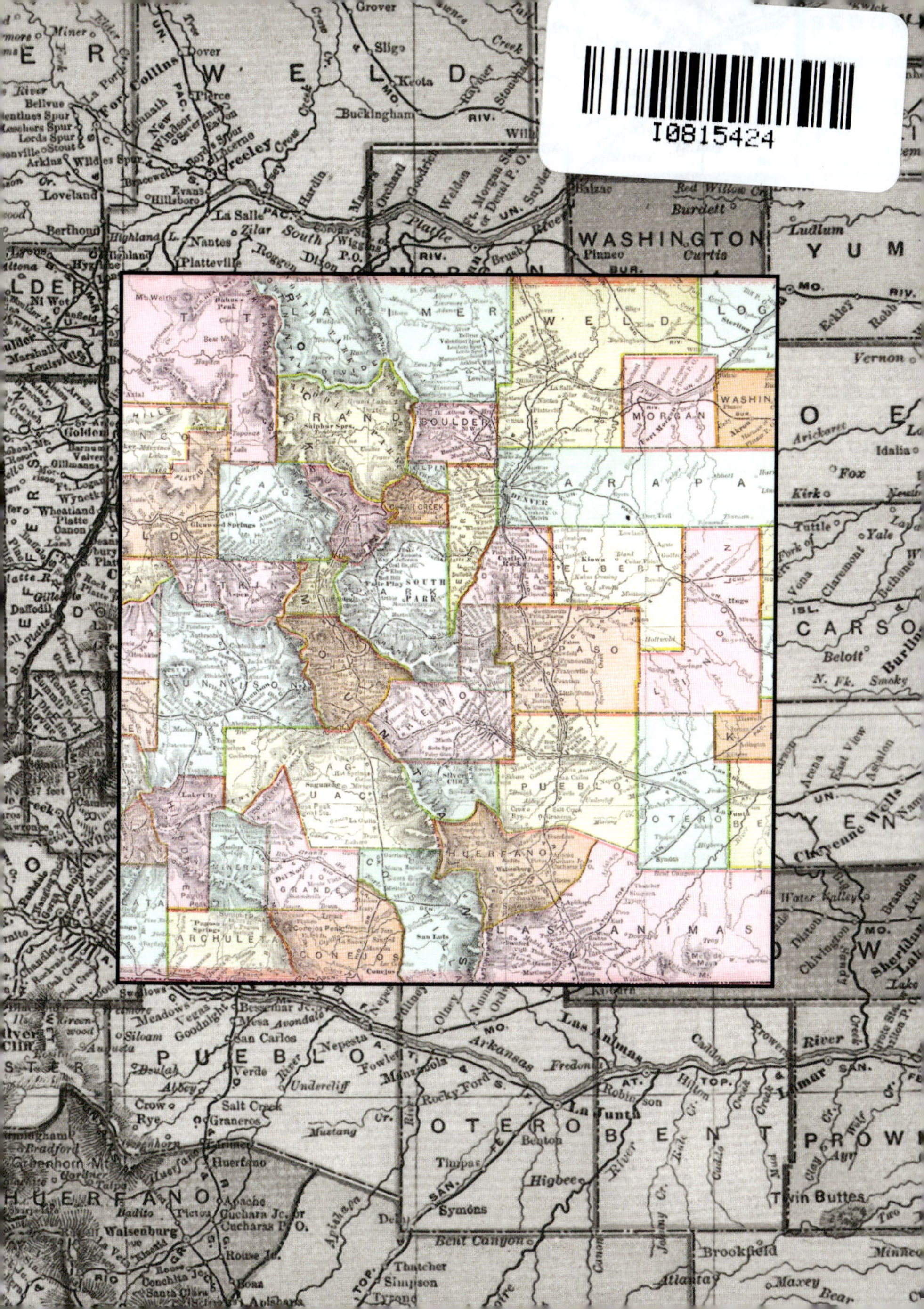
I0815424
WELD
WASHINGTON
Fort Collins
Greeley
Loveland
Denver
Golden
PUEBLO
OTERO
BENT
HUERFANO
La Junta
Walsenburg
Rocky Ford
Las Animas
Twin Buttes
Brookfield
CARSON
GRAND
BOULDER
ELBERT
EL PASO
PITKIN
GUNNISON
ARCHULETA
CONEJOS
LAS ANIMAS

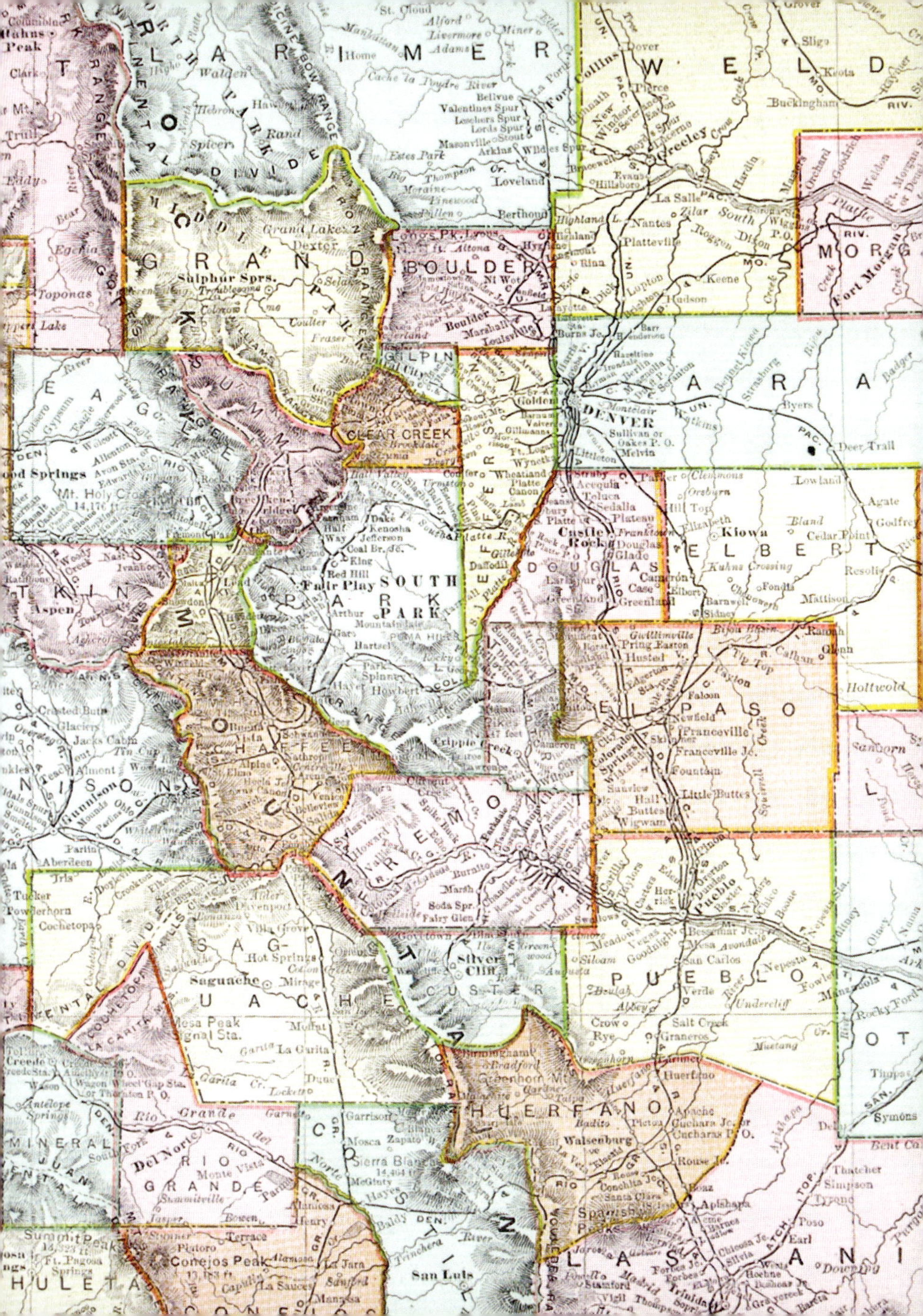

COLORADO COCKTAILS

A Collection of Over 100 Recipes from the Rocky Mountain State

AMANDA M. FAISON

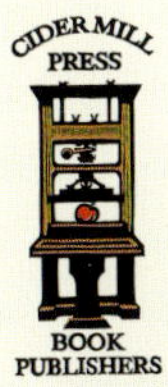

COLORADO COCKTAILS

13-Digit ISBN: 978-1-40034-627-1
10-Digit ISBN: 1-40034-627-4

Books published by Cider Mill Press Book Publishers are available at special discounts for bulk purchases in the United States by corporations, institutions, and other organizations. For more information, please contact the publisher.

Cider Mill Press Book Publishers
"Where good books are ready for press"
501 Nelson Place
Nashville, Tennessee 37214, USA

cidermillpress.com

HarperCollins Publishers, Macken House, 39/40 Mayor Street Upper, Dublin 1, D01 C9W8, Ireland (https://www.harpercollins.com)

Typography: Archive Antiqua Extra Cond, Copperplate, Sackers, Warnock

Photography credits on page 276

Printed in India

25 26 27 28 29 REP 5 4 3 2 1

First Edition

CONTENTS

Breckenridge

INTRODUCTION

Denver

Colorado's cocktail history is divided into two parts: Before Williams & Graham, and after Williams & Graham. The defining date—November 15, 2011—marks the moment that Sean Kenyon's 1920s-style bar opened at 32nd Avenue and Tejon Street in Denver. The bar didn't literally fling open its doors, but when the secret door (actually a bookshelf with a hidden lock) did first swing open, Williams & Graham sparked new energy into the city, and ultimately, the entire state.

The Big Bang: 2011, When the Cocktail Renaissance Arrived in Denver

"We can look at every major city in the flyover states and identify a bar and a person in each one of those cities where the cocktail renaissance kicked off," says Chad Michael George, a longtime Denver bartender and bar consultant. "They weren't the first, but they were the ones who were the fertilizer on the lawn and everything sprouted from there. [In Colorado,] that was Williams & Graham."

Kenyon's approach to hospitality was unique and foundational to the growth of Denver's cocktail scene. As Jason Patz, one of the bar's opening bartenders and now the beverage director for La Forêt, The Tatarian, Union Lodge No. 1, and The Arvada Tavern, says, "Williams & Graham helped define what a cocktail bar is."

Aside from Williams & Graham and another Denver speakeasy, Green Russell, finding an excellent cocktail in the state was no easy feat. There was Steuben's in uptown Denver, The Cruise Room for ice-cold martinis downtown, and The Bitter Bar in Boulder, but virtually nowhere else was pushing beyond your pre-renaissance night-out standards like Rum & Cokes, Red Bull & Vodkas, and Gin & Tonics. Even finding a cocktail menu at a restaurant (aside from the typical martini list at a steak house) was a novelty.

At the time, Colorado was firmly microbrew country. "When we arrived [in 2012], craft beer was king," says McLain Hedges. Hedges and his wife, Mary Allison Wright, opened RiNo Yacht Club at The Source, which later became Yacht Club in the Cole neighborhood and winner of the Best U.S. Cocktail Bar at the 2024 Tales of the Cocktail Foundation Spirited Awards. "That was Colorado—spirits were secondary, and wine was tertiary at best."

In more ways than one, 2011 marked an important time in Denver's bar history. With Williams & Graham, there was finally a venue that was equally enticing for the public and for hospitality industry insiders. Folks started coming just to try something new, be it a cocktail, a specific spirit, or just to feel part of something. "We opened our arms to bartenders from around the city, and people would come and just try things out," says Kenyon. He would stock rare bottles, like the extremely bitter orange peel liqueur Amer Picon, just for tasting. "It was like a bartender's Chipotle: 'Can you put this with that? And that with this?' They had never seen some of these things before. We were becoming that bar."

From this thinktank of sorts, excitement, knowledge, and talent radiated out. Today, many of the state's best bartenders were either inspired by or worked behind the bar at Williams & Graham. Some out-of-state transplants even shelved what they were doing elsewhere and moved to Colorado to seek Kenyon's tutelage. "One of the reasons we found ourselves in Colorado and why Yacht Club could work was Sean Kenyon," Wright says. "Our experience at Squeaky Bean [a lightning-in-a-bottle restaurant where Kenyon tended bar] is why we found ourselves here. Sean was accepting and mentoring to us."

Some Context: Prohibition's Legacy

Colorado Springs and Broadmoor Hotel in the distance, 1927

For so long, Colorado had a narrow vision of spirits. This is no doubt related to Prohibition, which went into effect on January 1, 1916, four years before the rest of the country. Even today, ripple effects remain in the form of bizarre and archaic liquor laws. "The fact that Colorado was a prohibitive market for so long," George explains, "means those remnants of conservative stances on liquor are still in our laws and are harmful to the industry as a whole."

Some examples: Liquor only became available for sale on Sundays starting in 2008; prior to 2009, beer sold in grocery stores could not exceed 3.2% ABV; (for better or worse) wine only just made its way into select Colorado grocery stores in 2023; and the ban on Christmas Day alcohol sales was only lifted in 2024.

The resurgence of the state's cocktail culture was a slow process, with a steep learning curve. At first, at some bars, the experience was intentionally mysterious and arrogant. "The cocktail industry had given the impression that your drink is going to take twenty minutes and the bartender is not going to be friendly," Kenyon says. "I didn't want that."

In 2014, Sean Kenyon won Best American Bartender at Tales of the Cocktail in New Orleans—the highest mixology honor on the planet. Bartenders all over the world took notice. The little bar that could ("I didn't know if we would last a year," Kenyon says now) was making huge waves in the middle of the country. That effort was further rewarded when, at Tales a year later, Williams & Graham was awarded Best American Cocktail Bar. (You'd better believe that there's a correlation between Williams & Graham's success and Death & Co opening its Denver outpost in 2018.) Perhaps the most meaningful accolade came in 2022 when Kenyon was named Best U.S. Bar Mentor, also at Tales of the Cocktail. Kenyon puts it like this: "I always wanted to own a bar that takes care of its own."

Colorado Cocktail Trend 1: NA and Low-ABV Mocktails

In recent years, it's a fair bet that one of the biggest trends in cocktails is the growth of zero-proof and low-alcohol drinks (there are some recipes sprinkled throughout this book). And while this is true in Colorado, Alex Jump, the former bar manager for Death & Co Denver and co-owner of the soon-to-open Peach Crease Club, says, "In general there's a huge demand, but I get the feeling that Denver is more of a drinking town." Stuart Jensen, Jump's husband and the other half of Peach Crease Club, agrees: "Other cities have people who are long-term sober going out as sober people. Denver is more short-term sober."

That said, this observation varies depending on where you sit. Jensen, who is also co-owner of Curio Bar at Denver Central Market in RiNo and Roger's Liquid Oasis at Edgewater Public Market in Edgewater, says that Curio doesn't see much in the way of NA orders, but there's a fair amount of interest at Roger's. Meanwhile, Caroline Clark, director of beverage and hospitality for Id Est Hospitality, which owns Michelin-starred Brutø and Wolf's Tailor as well as Hey Kiddo, OK Yeah, and others, firmly believes that zero-proof is a critical part of any bar program. "When you don't have something NA listed, the odds of people asking for something go way down. But once you invest in a program, all of these people come out of the woodwork," she says.

George, for one, doesn't totally love the low-ABV trend, if only because those who order low-alcohol drinks don't usually also consider their volume. "An Aperol Spritz is just as boozy as a margarita," he says. "If I see a low ABV, I immediately start doing the math, and very rarely are they low ABV." Some bars report seeing a rise in zero-proof drinks spiked with a shot of vodka or whiskey. "You can get super crafty with mocktail to cocktail," says Juan Padró, CEO of the Culinary Creative Group, which owns multiple Denver restaurants and bars, including Forget Me Not, Ay Papi, and Hello Gorgeous. "We're seeing a lot of people ordering a mocktail with a shot of vodka. Two things: They're delicious and they can control the amount of alcohol."

Meanwhile, up in the mountains, zero-proof and low-ABV cocktails appear on menus, but the general consensus is that when people visit resort towns, they are there to treat themselves. "People are on vacation and cocktails are part of that experience," says Hannah Hopkins, chef-owner of Yampa Valley Kitchen, Bésame, and Mambo in Steamboat Springs. Even so, she still appeals to the NA crowd with drinks like the Harvest Moon, but a bigger trend, she says, is drinks that are less sweet and more savory. Hopkins' most popular cocktail at Besamé is the Tipsy Carrot, which is a play on the margarita but with carrot juice.

Colorado Cocktail Trend 2: Savory Cocktails

Savory cocktails now reach far, far beyond the realm of Bloody Marys or Dirty Martinis. Patz has a Cornichon Spritz and a celery-forward cocktail called the Duke of Mirepoix on La Forêt's menu. At Lady Jane, bartender Danny Garcia messed around with the quintessential flavors of tacos al pastor until he perfected the Con Todo, complete with corn tortilla–infused mezcal. MAKfam bar manager, Grace Tomczak has a gin cocktail highlighting and celebrating the umami-beauty of MSG.

Fat-washing is having its moment too. This method of imparting flavor and mouthfeel has made it into the mainstream with duck fat-washed Old Fashioneds and Manhattans hitting restaurant menus. "We always have something that's clarified or fat-washed," says Billie

Keithley, liquid chef at Breckenridge Distillery in Breckenridge. "It's fun to explain to a guest when they ask, 'What does this mean?'. It's a great talking point." And to their credit, home bartenders are significantly more fluent in bartender speak after experimenting and building their personal bars during the pandemic. Some think nothing of infusing a spirit with butter or bacon grease—techniques that used to quietly live behind the bar.

Colorado Cocktail Trend 3: Casual Concepts

If one thing stands out in Colorado's evolving industry, it's how democratized cocktails have become. Once solely the domain of high-end cocktail bars, bartending knowledge and talent has trickled down to the point where nearly every restaurant now has at least a decent curated drink menu. "What I love is that the rocket ship that became craft cocktails in late 2000s and 2010s has spun out to upscale casual and fine-dining restaurants. Everyone got in the game," George says. This is certainly true on the bar front too. "There's a move to more casual drinking concepts, things that are less stuffy. Yacht Club is a good example," Jump says.

The key is meeting people where they're at, something that has been a focus of Kenyon's since he opened Williams & Graham—and certainly was a guiding force behind Occidental, the casual neighborhood bar he opened next door to W&G in 2015. This will be true again when Kenyon debuts a new venue at Denver International Airport in February 2025. If that seems like a departure from all that Kenyon has built, he disagrees. "We've always wanted buzz and movement," he says. And travelers will still have to find it: the bar isn't set out in the open in the A Concourse; it's tucked away and intimate.

Stocking the Ultimate Colorado Bar

Want to show off your Colorado cocktail prowess? Build your bar around these local products.

Tipsy Jigger: When the pandemic hit, Denver resident and CBS motion graphic designer Chad Roark had time on his hands. He took an interest in an antique rollover jigger inherited from his father-in-law. The bar tool was beautiful and meaningful but very fragile, and Roark wanted to recreate it. Before long, he was watching YouTube videos, buying metal-working machinery, and turning his basement into a full-fledged work-shop. He learned by trial and error and in 2024 he began selling two handcrafted models—the Nick and the Nora, named after characters in *The Thin Man*. The differences are subtle but with either design, home bartenders will appreciate the bell shape, the precise measurements (starting at a quarter of an ounce all the way up to two ounces), and the ease of tipping spirits directly into the glass.

Laradacky: Aesthetics count when it comes to setting up the home bar, so don't muck up the look with a plastic cutting board. Instead, invest in a Laradacky. These gorgeously crafted serving boards are the work of Denver furniture designer David Larabee and his wife, interior designer Megan Hudacky. The boards are the definition of functional beauty, and they transfer beautifully from bar to table.

DRAM Apothecary: What first began as an attempt at making wild mountain sage bitters from a recipe in an M.F.K. Fisher novel, has grown into a full-fledged business. With foraged ingredients from the wilds of Colorado, Shae Whitney and Brady Becker make bitters, switchels (similar to a shrub), adaptogenic sparkling waters, and Colorado Pine Syrup. Their business first took root when they opened Bread Bar in Silver Plume, but has since expanded and moved to Salida. The bitters are pure in flavor and alcohol-free, but the real winner is the pine syrup, which absolutely erupts in a cocktail like a Gin & Tonic or even a Manhattan.

DRAM'S ALPINE MANHATTAN

GLASSWARE: Martini glass

GARNISH: Brandied cherry or orange peel

- 1½ oz. bourbon
- 1 oz. DRAM Colorado Pine Syrup
- 5 shakes DRAM Black Bitters

1. Chill a martini glass. Combine all of the ingredients in a mixing glass or cocktail shaker. Add ice and stir or shake.
2. Strain the cocktail into a chilled martini glass and garnish with a brandied cherry or orange peel.

LEOPOLD BROS: Leopold Bros' line of spirits is so impressive that one could be forgiven in thinking that the distillery is a big operation. Au contraire. Todd and Scott Leopold are devoted to the craft of small-batch spirits, and that quality shows, be it in the whiskies (don't miss the Maryland Rye), the liqueurs (sub the Aperitivo Classico for Campari), or the gins. Fans anxiously await the release of Leopold's Summer Gin, a fresh blend that drinks of the season and varies slightly every year. In particular, the Navy Strength Gin is so clean, smooth, and strong that it's dangerously good—and a must on any backbar.

STRONGWATER: When mixologist, herbalist, and chemist Nicholas Andresen was growing up, the answer to most any ailment was an herbal remedy. He learned their value from his Scandinavian and Korean grandparents, and when he married a sommelier named Asha, the two put their heads together to create Strongwater. What emerged was a line of artisanal, exquisitely flavored bitters that shunned sugar. Many awards later, the company has grown to include a line of cocktail syrups, sparkling mixers, and sodas.

Law's Whiskey: Small-batch whiskey is founder Al Laws' religion. And thus it makes sense that Law's Whiskey House has a tasting room with a church-like space, complete with wooden pews and cathedral windows. The name of said space: The Sanctuary. Here, patrons can sip the Colorado-grain-driven whiskey by the cocktail, pour, or flight. Of course, there are also bottles to purchase to take home, of which you should consider the Bonded Centennial Straight Wheat Whiskey. This limited-release beauty is made from heirloom soft white spring wheat grown from the San Luis Valley. It's also the first Colorado-made wheat whiskey to meet the standards of the Bottled in Bond Act of 1897, meaning it was "produced at a single distillery during a single distilling season, aged for at least four years, and bottled at 100 proof."

Peach Street Distillers: Most people first discover Peach Street through its wonderfully smooth Colorado-made bourbon, but that's really just the gateway drug. The distillery, which is based in Palisade—the epicenter of Colorado orchard country—has become best known for its mind-blowingly good brandies and eaux-de-vie—peach, apricot, pear, plum, and cherry. A note of quality: To make a single (750 ml) bottle of this peach brandy, it takes twenty-six pounds of Palisade peaches and six years in French Oak. The underlying message is that, at Peach Street, perfection takes time.

Woody Creek Distillers: Friends Patrick Scanlan and Mark Kleckner started Woody Creek Distillers both as a hobby (they're retired engineers who worked for the Department of Defense) and a reaction to the nastiness that is often mainstream vodka. Most conventional vodkas are made from distilled neutral grain spirit (NGS), which is industrial-grade ethanol made in refineries and delivered by the tanker truck. Woody Creek's vodka, so named for the unincorporated Gonzo-esque town made famous by Hunter S. Thompson, crafts vodka in the Roaring Fork Valley from a mix of Stobrawa and Rio Grande potatoes. It's expensive to make and costs a little more to drink, but it goes down like velvet.

The Decc Citrus Clove Liqueur: This concoction came about by accident. When Distillery 291's founding distiller (and former New York fashion photographer) Michael Myers was working a cold-weather whiskey event, he quickly whipped up a tasting blend of whiskey, citrus, and clove for festivalgoers. The sip was such a hit that Myers knew he was onto something. Buy a bottle and add a dash to a hot toddy, a flask of whiskey, or an Old Fashioned.

Uncle Tim's Cocktails: Founders Tim Felkner and Patrick Stern partner with small-batch Colorado distillers to create 750-milliliter bottles of ready-to-drink (RTD) cocktails such as Black Walnut Manhattans, Boulevardiers, and Negronis. The drinks stand on their own, or can be mixed to create entirely new cocktails.

CapRock Gin: Haters insist that, as a rule, gin is too juniper-y or too pine-y (or too both), but not CapRock. This handcrafted spirit from Jack Rabbit Hill Farm in Hotchkiss is a certified organic treasure. Made with Jonathan and Braeburn apples grown at nearby Ela Family Farms, the gin is floral, delicate, and speaks of an operation that leans on first-use irrigation water, rich soil, exquisitely farmed fruit, and the magic that happens in a little copper still.

Bonus: While perusing Colorado liquor stores, if you come across any bottle from the recently closed Golden Moon Distillery, buy it. Stephen Gould's spirits were impeccably researched, crafted in small batches, and some of the very best anywhere. A real find: the sweet, creamy, and slightly bitter crème de violette, made with distilled violets.

Basic Preparations and Techniques

Shake or wet shake: Add ingredients and ice to a cocktail tin and shake it. This simultaneously chills, dilutes, and mixes the drink.

Dry shake: Add just the ingredients—no ice—to a cocktail tin and shake. The technique is often used with cocktails containing egg whites or aquafaba to create a silky froth.

Whip shake: A quick shake with only a couple pieces of ice creates a lightly diluted, aerated cocktail.

Fine strain and double strain: These terms are used interchangeably to indicate when a cocktail needs to be strained twice—once through a Hawthorne strainer (the one with the springs) and again through a small, usually conical fine-mesh strainer.

Simple Syrup: This mixture of sugar water is used as a sweetener. Simple syrup can also be infused with a variety of ingredients, such as basil, cardamom, or lemongrass. To make it, combine equal parts sugar with water, bring the mixture to a low simmer, stir until the sugar is dissolved, remove from heat, and cool. Refrigerate for up to one month. To make a rich simple syrup, use two parts sugar to one part water. To make a demerara syrup, use demerara sugar instead of white sugar. To make a rich demerara syrup, double the sugar relative to the water.

Honey Syrup: Used as a substitute for simple syrup, honey syrup is a diluted mixture of honey and water. To make it, combine two parts honey with one part water (1 cup honey to ½ cup water, for example), bring to a low simmer, stir until the honey is dissolved, remove from heat, and cool. Alternatively, pour boiling water into honey and stir. Refrigerate for up to one month.

Saline Solution: As with food, salt can make a cocktail's flavors pop, and this mixture of salt and water does just that. (In all fairness, most bartenders say a small pinch of salt will have the same effect.) To make a 10% saline solution, combine one part salt to nine parts hot water (i.e., 10 grams salt and 90 grams water) and stir until the salt is dissolved. To make a 20% solution, use two parts salt to eight parts water. Refrigerate for up to one month.

Express: The process of twisting a citrus peel—orange, lemon, or lime—over a cocktail to release the citrus oils and essences into the glass. (This is not the same as squeezing juice into a cocktail.)

The Dos and Don'ts of Drinking Like a Local

- **Do** make a pilgrimage to Williams & Graham to better understand the origin story of Colorado cocktail culture.
- Want to say you're an out-of-towner without saying you're an out-of-towner? **Do** order a Colorado Bulldog, basically a White Russian with Coke.
- **Don't** go skiing or snowboarding at Arapahoe Basin and not order the legendary Bacon Bloody Mary. Given how many they serve in a season—more than 30,000—the cocktail could be considered Colorado's signature cocktail.

DENVER

Blackberry Sage Smash
Time & Place
Alabaster
Circuit Breaker
Cornichon Spritz
Duke of Mirepoix
Union Gin Fizz
Knickerbocker
Tatarian
Circus
Tavernetta Negroni
Guilty Pleasures
MSGin
Hiss Hiss Bang Bang
Haute Box
The Yellow Cocktail
Duck Old Fashioned
Mistah Bittah Hai
Mai Tai
Con Todo
Expeditions
Lava Mama
Easy Lover
8 AM
The Green Hour
Wild Fashion
Easy Sailor

Bomba Rosa
Princetonian
Striptease Falcon
Fantômas
Peacewalker
Green Tomato Gimlet
Dockside
Howling Wolf
No. 3
Albatross
Kogani no Mori
Beach Don't Kill My Vibe
Red Skies at Night
Whiskey Mango Foxtrot
Fire on the Li River
Dirty Deeds
Ginger Lyte (NA)
Quetzalcoatl
Oh My Lört
Cherry
Ded Reckoning
Changes in Attitude
Silent Disco
Kyoto Lemonade
The Wildflower
Bergamot Toddy
El Chufacabra

Even those who haven't been to Denver know its nickname: The Mile High City. Find your way to the granite steps of the State Capitol building, and you'll see "one mile above sea level" chiseled into the fifteenth step. And, yes, you might also see a brass plaque on the eighteenth and thirteenth steps . . . the demarcation has been moved through the years as surveying technology has gotten more precise. No matter; you can rest assured that somewhere around there—and in many parts of the city—you're officially standing at a mile high.

The thing folks will tell you about Denver is that it feels more like a big town than a big city. Sure, the population of the entire metro area is three million, but Denver proper is roughly 715,000. All of which is to say, the city is big but it isn't *that* big. Still, it is, of course, the capital of Colorado, and the state's largest metropolis.

You can assume Denver's low-key, friendly vibe (it remains the pioneering West, where people come to reinvent themselves) and proximity to the Rocky Mountains are the primary reasons for the city's growth spurt. To wit, Denver's population grew more than nineteen percent between 2010 and 2020. But with more people come more ideas, more diversity, and more jumping-off points that translate into exciting upticks in food, beverage, and cultural trends.

SEAN KENYON, WILLIAMS & GRAHAM AND OCCIDENTAL

Although the godfather of Denver's cocktail scene didn't know it at the time, a simple request for a classic cocktail would change everything—for him and for Colorado. "I was working the bar at Steuben's when a friend who was a rep for Jim Beam asked me for a Manhattan," Sean Kenyon says. "I shook the shit out of that Manhattan. He looked at me all weird and said, 'No one in Denver does any classic cocktail well.'"

That was 2009-ish, when Kenyon was already a career bartender. He was speedy and he knew menu drinks, but he didn't know classic cocktails. No one he knew (or, frankly, anyone under the age of eighty) was sipping a stirred cocktail unless it was a Martini. Kenyon and the rep talked the recipe through and Kenyon made another, this time stirred. "I remade it, tasted it, and was like, 'Holy shit,'" he recalls.

Immediately after, he dove deep into cocktail history and never looked back. "I remember thinking, 'I've been doing this for twenty years,'" Kenyon says. "'How come I don't know everything about this industry?'"

Kenyon bounced his new-found knowledge off of anyone who would listen. He taught Randy Layman (who was bartending at The Avenue Grill across the street and would take over as Steuben's bar manager when Kenyon left in 2010) how to make a Vieux Carré so he could drink them. He wrote a new menu for Steuben's—one where the right things were shaken and the right things were stirred. He wasn't sure if Steuben's clientele would glom on (or even care) but they loved it. Denver's burgeoning cocktail movement was officially in motion.

Kenyon, who is from New Jersey, is a barman through and through. His father and grandfather owned bars and took pride in working behind the stick. Kenyon grew up in bars, and he cherishes the place they occupy in the community. He also loves the role a bartender plays because it's so much more than just slinging drinks. "Bartenders string everything together," he says. "I teach our team that the lone guest is your most important guest. They're not just coming for a drink; they're coming to be part of a community."

And that degree of hospitality is exactly what Kenyon gave to Denver in 2011 when he opened Williams & Graham, a Prohibition-style speakeasy hidden behind a bookshop in LoHi. Of course, there were other bars in Denver before Williams & Graham, but none were as steeped in the spirit of hospitality or as deeply committed to uncovering cocktail knowledge. Williams & Graham sought to create a cocktail *experience*.

In 2014, just three years after opening, Williams & Graham had landed on *Drinks International* magazine's "World's Top 50 Bars" list, and Kenyon won Bartender of the year at Tales of the Cocktail. The following year, Williams & Graham won the highest honor in the land when it was named American Cocktail Bar of the Year at Tales of the Cocktail Foundation Spirited Awards. The awards are gravy, but at the end of the day, Kenyon's goal remains creating spaces in which people want to gather.

BLACKBERRY SAGE SMASH

WILLIAMS & GRAHAM
3160 TEJON STREET, DENVER

The Blackberry Sage Smash has been a staple on Williams & Graham's menu since the very beginning. The drink underscores owner Sean Kenyon's belief that a simple cocktail is often more difficult to pull off than a more complicated one because there's nothing to hide behind. He also likes having something on the menu that isn't intimidating. "The flagship cocktail has to be accessible and make sense to people," Kenyon says. "It's something people can revisit every single time they come, and that familiarity breeds trust and allows people to branch out to the rest of the menu."

GLASSWARE: Double rocks glass

GARNISH: Fresh sage leaf and blackberry speared on a toothpick

- **4 sage leaves**
- **4 blackberries**
- **2 oz. Knob Creek 9 Year Bourbon Whiskey**
- **½ oz. Simple Syrup (see recipe on page 18)**
- **¼ oz. fresh lemon juice**

1. Muddle 4 sage leaves and 4 blackberries in a cocktail shaker tin.
2. Add the remaining ingredients with ice and shake.
3. Strain the cocktail into a double rocks glass over ice and garnish with a fresh sage leaf and blackberry speared on a toothpick.

TYSON BUHLER AND MAGGIE SANDERS, DEATH & CO DENVER

Death & Co is a bar so legendary its reputation precedes it. And even if a bar enthusiast hasn't sipped a finely crafted cocktail within its walls (there are locations in New York, Denver, Los Angeles, Washington, DC, and soon Seattle), they likely have the bar's books, *Death & Co, Cocktail Codex*, and *Death & Co: Welcome Home* displayed on their bookshelves. The original bar opened in Manhattan in 2006 and quickly established itself as a giant among twenty-first-century cocktail renaissance legends like PDT and Milk and Honey. And, then, in 2018, Death & Co made a shocking decision to a) expand and b) expand to Denver. It was a head-scratching move, but one that was prescient, as its location in the lobby of Denver's Ramble Hotel has both retained and built on the original's magic. Here is Tyson Buhler, Death & Co's national director of food and beverage, and Maggie Sanders, Death & Co Denver general manager, in their own words.

Why, of all the cities, did Death & Co choose Denver as its second location?

Tyson Buhler: Denver was a city that had already established itself with plenty of great bars and restaurants, but was also in a period of huge growth. Getting to come in and learn and grow alongside the rest of the city was a really exciting opportunity for us. We knew early on we couldn't take what we'd done in New York and create a carbon copy in another city. The inherent culture of a place is needed to shape the success of a bar, so it would have been almost easier, in a sense, to take a bigger leap for the first outpost than to try and open in a city that maybe has more similarity to NYC, like Chicago or Los Angeles.

What role does the bar play in the Denver scene?

TB: Six years in, the bar is really entrenched in the community. It's a place that so much of the industry in the Denver community has interacted with in some way. They may have worked here for a period of time, been to one of the many seminars or pop-ups we've hosted, or just frequented the bar on their nights off.

Does D&C have any part-time bartenders who moonlight elsewhere, or only full-timers?

Maggie Sanders: Many of our bartenders are full time, but we have a handful who hold positions at other bars in Denver as a way of continuing to hone their skills. For example, a D&C bartender has incredible knowledge of hospitality and spirits, but our structured and controlled service rarely pushes them to the point of chaos. Many of them want to stay fast in the wells, contribute to the Denver bar scene by sharing their techniques, participate in competitions, and learn different methods of service.

TB: Great bar teams are a made up of people with a diverse set of skills and experiences and this current team, as with so many others who have graced this bar, does just that. I love when we have staff that works shifts at other bars. They bring a different viewpoint and help us continue to reevaluate the way we do things.

TIME & PLACE

DEATH & CO
1280 25TH STREET, DENVER

Time & Place was intended to be a winter Manhattan-style cocktail for sipping in front of the fire. Using Cocchi Rosa as the fortified wine element, this cocktail takes the usual deep rich flavors you expect in a Manhattan and pushes it into lighter red fruit and florals. A high-proof spirit is necessary to balance the sweetness of the fortified wines, and the Stellum fits the bill perfectly. A small amount of eau de vie roots the cocktail with an earthy finishing note. The result is a Manhattan that is warming and boozy but with underlying seasonal notes of cranberry, roasted root vegetables, and baking spices.

GLASSWARE: Nick & Nora glass
GARNISH: Lemon twist

- 1¼ oz. Stellum Bourbon
- 1 oz. Taylor Fladgate 10 Year Old Tawny Port
- ¾ oz. Cocchi Rosa
- 1 teaspoon Reisetbauer Carrot Eau de Vie
- 2 dashes The Bitter Truth Old Time Aromatic Bitters

1. Chill a Nick & Nora glass. Combine all of the ingredients in a chilled mixing tin.
2. Add ice and stir until very cold.
3. Strain the cocktail into the chilled Nick & Nora and garnish with a lemon twist.

ALABASTER

DEATH & CO
1280 25TH STREET, DENVER

Inspired by a night out with friends, former Death & Co Denver bar manager Jake Powell's Alabaster is a refreshing patio-pounder meant for Colorado's summers. Cucumber and mint's freshness abound in this take on a Last Word. Bright and citrusy, this is one that'll go down all too easily during the dog days of summer.

GLASSWARE: Nick & Nora glass

- **¾ oz. Probitas Rum**
- **¾ oz. Chareau**
- **¾ oz. John D. Taylor's Velvet Falernum**
- **¾ oz. fresh lime juice**

1. Chill a Nick & Nora glass. Combine all of the ingredients in a cocktail shaker tin.
2. Add ice and shake until very cold.
3. Double-strain the cocktail into the chilled Nick & Nora.

CIRCUIT BREAKER

DEATH & CO
1280 25TH STREET, DENVER

The universe works in mysterious ways. Shortly after bartender Jack Stevenson first tasted Nixta, a Mexican corn liqueur, the spirit came up in a conversation with a customer. As he explains it, he was chatting with a guest from Mexico, who mentioned his love for mezcal and Montenegro shots. "He then talked about how he had added Nixta to the mix and adjusted it to be closer to an Old Fashioned," says Stevenson. That interaction inspired Stevenson to create his own version and, thus, the Circuit Breaker came into focus.

GLASSWARE: Rocks glass
GARNISH: Orange twist

- **1 oz. Mezcal Vago Elote**
- **½ oz. Uruapan Charanda Añejo Rum**
- **½ oz. Nixta Licor de Elote**
- **¼ oz. Cynar**
- **Dash Angostura bitters**

1. Combine all of the ingredients in a chilled mixing glass.
2. Add ice and stir until the ingredients are incorporated and just slightly chilled.
3. Strain the cocktail over a large ice cube and garnish with an orange twist.

JASON PATZ , LA FORÊT, THE TATARIAN, UNION LODGE NO. 1, AND THE ARVADA TAVERN

If you've hung around Denver's bar scene for any length of time, Jason Patz's name has likely surfaced. A native of Albuquerque, Patz has worked in the industry since he was thirteen. The truth is, Patz is first and foremost an artist (he came to Denver in 1999 to pursue a degree in drawing and painting from Rocky Mountain Institute of Art & Design). On the side, Patz spent time in Denver bars and restaurants and eventually landed a job as a national trainer for P.F. Chang's. After several years, he grew weary of the job's harried schedule, and decided he wanted to return to Denver's bar scene.

At the time, Sean Kenyon was getting ready to open Williams & Graham, the LoHi cocktail bar that would fundamentally launch Denver's—and Colorado's—craft cocktail scene (see the Introduction). "I followed Sean around and sat at all the bars he was working at, like Squeaky Bean and Euclid Hall. I sat in front of him until he gave me a job," Patz says. When Williams & Graham debuted in 2011, Patz was one of the opening bartenders. About a year in, he took over as bar manager and, in total, he spent five years working with Kenyon. (Patz also helped Kenyon open Occidental in 2015.) To say Patz was part of something big is an understatement.

But burnout was real, and after years of working long hours and late nights, Patz took a step back. But he didn't go far: He continued to help friends open bars and restaurants and did a stint with chef Jeff Osaka when Twelve Restaurant moved from downtown to Congress Park. Patz even moonlighted at his favorite neighborhood bar—Hudson Hill—when it was short staffed. In 2017, Mike Huggins and Lenka Juchelkova of The Arvada Tavern, Union Lodge No. 1, and the soon-to-launch Tatarian, approached him to come aboard as their beverage director.

Patz and the hospitality group, GuestFloor Management, weathered the pandemic and have since opened La Forêt, a cocktail bar and French restaurant, on South Broadway. As beverage director, Patz doesn't spend as much time as he used to behind the stick (though he still fills in), but his thumbprint is everywhere. He manages and runs the beverage programs, which means overseeing five to seven different menus at any given time.

Patz has never lost touch with the creative side of the business. "Cocktails are the original American culinary art," he explains. "Blending flavors, working with different spirits, and building something new and special, it's all an artform," he says. Ever the artist, Patz feeds the right side of his brain by both dreaming up cocktails and working in the small studio he's kept for two decades. "I'm always using a creative mindset," he says.

CORNICHON SPRITZ

LA FORÊT
38 SOUTH BROADWAY, DENVER

This spritz was created for La Forêt's pastis menu, otherwise known as the South Broadway bar's happy hour. The cocktail took shape as beverage director Jason Patz was researching French spirits. "Bigallet Thym Liqueur was one that really intrigued me," he says. "It was slightly sweet and savory all at the same time, and I knew I wanted to create a savory, light, refreshing Spritz with it."

GLASSWARE: Collins glass
GARNISH: Cornichons

- **1½ oz. Lillet Blanc**
- **½ oz. Bigallet Thym Liqueur**
- **¾ oz. Cucumber Tonic Syrup (see recipe)**
- **3 to 4 oz. soda water, to top**

1. Chill a collins glass. In the chilled glass, build the cocktail by adding the first three ingredients.
2. Add ice and top with soda water. Give it a little stir to combine.
3. Garnish with 1 or 2 cornichons.

Cucumber Tonic Syrup: Juice cucumbers, peeled and chopped, in a vegetable juicer until you have 2 cups of liquid. In a dry pan over medium heat, toast 1 oz. whole coriander seeds until fragrant. In a container, combine the cucumber juice; the toasted coriander; 1 oz. fresh lemon peel, cut into small pieces; and ¼ oz. thyme stems and leaves, roughly chopped, and allow the mixture to steep at room temperature for 15 to 20 minutes. Add 1 pound sugar, 28 grams malic acid powder, and 14 grams citric acid powder and stir to dissolve.

DUKE OF MIREPOIX

LA FORÊT
38 SOUTH BROADWAY, DENVER

Celery is, admittedly, a divisive vegetable, but for those who love those crunchy sticks, this cocktail is for you. "This was a process drink for me," says beverage director Jason Patz. "I've always loved Dr. Brown's Cel-Ray Soda, and I wanted to create a refreshing carbonated celery drink." Ultimately, Patz fiddled with a range of techniques before landing on a clarified milk punch that's force-carbonated and served over ice. Note: This batch recipe yields 12 to 15 servings, and for best results, you need a SodaStream (or something similar) for carbonation.

GLASSWARE: Collins glass
GARNISH: Celery ribbon

- **25 oz. (750 ml) Celery Cordial (see recipe)**
- **17 oz. (500 ml) Citadelle Original Gin**
- **14 oz. whole milk, chilled**

1. In a large glass bowl or similar container, combine the cordial and the gin, then add the milk and stir. Let the mixture sit for a few minutes.
2. Using a fine-mesh strainer lined with coffee filters or cheesecloth, strain the mixture into a clean container until it runs clear. This takes time (up to a whole day), and if you have room in your refrigerator, it's best to keep the mixture cold as it's straining.

3. Move the strainer to a second clean container and continue to strain. Do not discard the milk solids, as they help clarify the cocktail. Repeat this process with the cloudy strain from the first container until you've strained all the liquid and it is clear. Cover and refrigerate the mixture until ready to serve.
4. Pour the punch into a SodaStream bottle and carbonate it.
5. Fill a collins glass with pebble or crushed ice. Pour about 4 oz. of the carbonated punch over the ice into the glass.
6. Garnish with a celery ribbon.

Celery Cordial: In a large glass container, combine 16 oz. fresh celery juice; 12 oz. white sugar; 16.5 grams citric acid; 10 grams coriander seed, toasted; 8.25 grams malic acid; and 2 grams salt and stir to dissolve the powders. Let the solution sit for 20 to 30 minutes, and then strain.

UNION GIN FIZZ

UNION LODGE NO. 1
1543 CHAMPA STREET, DENVER

Union Lodge is a speakeasy-style cocktail bar in downtown Denver specializing in pre-Prohibition drinks. The menu is extensive but one offering to keep an eye out for is the Ramos Gin Fizz. This classic hails from New Orleans and was created by Henry C. Ramos who ran the Imperial Saloon in the late 1800s. In its original state, the Ramos Gin Fizz is incredibly laborious, requiring a bartender to shake the cocktail for fifteenish minutes. Rest assured, this rendition is easier and faster, and adds a little bit of rounded fruitiness thanks to the berry tincture and sloe gin.

GLASSWARE: Collins glass

GARNISH: Metal straw threaded with fresh blackberry

- 1 oz. Hayman's Old Tom Gin
- 1 oz. Hayman's Sloe Gin
- ¾ oz. fresh lemon juice
- ¾ oz. Simple Syrup (see recipe on page 18)
- 2 oz. heavy cream
- 1 oz. Egg White Preparation (see recipe)
- 4 dashes orange flower water
- 2 dashes Vanilla Tincture (see recipe)
- 2 dashes Berry Tincture (see recipe)
- 1½ to 2½ oz. soda water, chilled

1. Chill a collins glass. Combine all of the ingredients, except for the soda water, in a cocktail shaker with ice and shake.

2. Strain off the ice and vigorously re-shake without ice in the same tin, to aerate the egg white and cream.
3. Add chilled soda water to the chilled collins glass.
4. Pour one-quarter to one-third of the shaken cocktail into the glass.
5. Wait 1 to 2 minutes for the initial pour to settle. Use a straw to poke a hole down the center of the foam on top of the drink, then slowly pour the rest of the cocktail into that hole.
6. Using tongs or tweezers, slowly guide the straw with the threaded blackberry into the hole.

Egg White Preparation: Place 1 egg white (or more if you're preparing a batch) in a shallow mixing bowl. Whip with a whisk or an immersion blender so that no clumps remain. The key is emulsification, not soft peaks.

Vanilla Tincture: Cut a lengthwise slit down a vanilla bean. Using the flat side of the knife, scrape out the tiny seeds. In a small container or mason jar, combine the cut vanilla bean and seeds and 8 to 12 oz. vodka or Everclear and let the infusion sit for 1 to 3 weeks, shaking every couple of days after about a month. Strain and transfer the tincture to a dasher bottle and store it in a cool, dark place indefinitely.

Berry Tincture: In a large container, combine 1 pound frozen mixed berries and 1 liter vodka or Everclear and let the infusion sit for 1 to 3 weeks. Strain, pour the tincture into a dasher bottle, and store it in the refrigerator for up to 1 month.

KNICKERBOCKER

UNION LODGE NO. 1
1543 CHAMPA STREET, DENVER

The Knickerbocker appeared in *The Bon Vivant's Companion,* one of the first American Cocktail books, written in 1862 by Jerry Thomas, a prolific celebrity bartender who worked all over the United States but was mostly based in New York and San Francisco. (He also spent some time here in Colorado.) Union Lodge took some liberty and adjusted the recipe to make it unique. The cocktail still has the original rum, raspberry, curaçao, and citrus; the bar just added a little prosecco to liven it up a bit.

GLASSWARE: Large coupe glass
GARNISH: Orchid

- **1½ oz. Bacardí Reserva Ocho**
- **½ oz. Giffard Triple Sec**
- **½ oz. Raspberry Syrup (see recipe)**
- **½ oz. fresh lemon juice**
- **1½ oz. prosecco, to top**

1. Combine all of the ingredients, except for the prosecco, in a cocktail shaker with ice and shake.
2. Strain the cocktail into a large coupe glass and top with prosecco.
3. Garnish with an orchid.

RASPBERRY SYRUP: Combine 12 oz. hot water and 3 oz. raspberries in a blender and blend on low. With the blender running, add 12 oz. sugar and blend, allowing the sugar to dissolve. Strain and store the syrup in the refrigerator for up to 2 weeks.

UNION LODGE
№1
AN AMERICAN BAR

TATARIAN

THE TATARIAN
4024 TENNYSON STREET, DENVER

The Tatarian, a contemporary cocktail bar, sits smack in the middle of Denver's Berkeley neighborhood. As the area was growing and gentrifying, a land- and home-developer would give people a tree to plant on their newly purchased property. Some of these trees were Tatarian maples, which became the bar's namesake.

GLASSWARE: Double rocks glass
GARNISH: Lemon peel

- **2 oz. 100-proof bourbon**
- **¼ oz. Amaro Montenegro**
- **¼ oz. Maple Lapsang Syrup (see recipe)**
- **2 dashes The Bitter Truth Jerry Thomas' Own Decanter Bitters**

1. Combine all of the ingredients in a mixing glass with ice and stir.
2. Strain the cocktail over a large cube of fresh ice and garnish with a lemon peel.

MAPLE LAPSANG SYRUP: Boil 8 oz. water in a saucepan. Remove the pan from heat and add ¼ oz. loose-leaf lapsang souchong tea, then steep for 5 to 8 minutes. Strain then combine the tea with 16 oz. Grade B maple syrup and stir to combine. Store, refrigerated, for up to 1 month.

CIRCUS

THE TATARIAN
4024 TENNYSON STREET, DENVER

Trees of all forms—be it different species or famous stands from around the world—are the inspiration for The Tatarian's cocktail menu. The Circus is so named for a special group of trees at Gilroy Gardens Theme Park in Gilroy, California. The "Circus Trees" are the result of grafting techniques by Axel Erlandson from the 1920s. Erlandson shaped sycamores into whimsical forms, creating a unique collection of sculpted trees.

GLASSWARE: Footed pilsner glass
GARNISH: Lime Peel Ribbon (see recipe), fancy orchid

- **2 oz. reposado tequila**
- **¾ oz. fresh lime juice**
- **¾ oz. Mango-Chile Agave Syrup (see recipe)**
- **¼ oz. Luxardo Bitter Bianco**
- **¼ oz. Small Hand Foods Passion Fruit Syrup**
- **Soda water, to top**

1. Combine all of the ingredients, except for the soda water, in a shaker tin with ice and shake.
2. Strain the cocktail over fresh ice into a footed pilsner glass.
3. Top with soda water and garnish with a lime peel ribbon and fancy orchid.

Mango-Chile Agave Syrup: Steep 1 oz. Maui Mango Tiesta Tea in 16 oz. just-boiled hot water for 8 to 10 minutes. Add 2 grams dried chile de árbol pods, crushed, and steep for another 5 to 8 minutes. Strain then add 8 oz. agave nectar and stir.

Lime Peel Ribbon: With a vegetable peeler, pull thin strips from lime peels. Wrap the peels around a straw or chopstick like curlicues. Place the curlicues in a dehydrator and dehydrate at medium heat for 30 to 45 minutes, until the ribbons hold their shape.

ERNETT

TAVERNETTA NEGRONI

TAVERNETTA
1889 16TH STREET, DENVER

Tavernetta's house Negroni recipe has been a staple since Frasca Hospitality Group made the leap to Denver in 2017 and opened the high-end Italian restaurant near Union Station. What sets this Negroni apart from others is a split base of two different vermouths—Carpano Antica, a rich, powerful expression of sweet vermouth with notes of dried fruit, vanilla, citrus, spice, and cacao; and Punt e Mes, a unique offering of vermouth that has a distinct bitterness derived from quinine. When it comes to Campari, there is simply no substitute. Meanwhile, St. George Botanivore is a layered, complex, and herbaceous gin with nineteen botanicals and notes of citrus and warm spice.

GLASSWARE: Rocks glass
GARNISH: Orange twist

- **1 oz. St. George Botanivore Gin**
- **1 oz. Campari**
- **½ oz. Punt e Mes**
- **½ oz. Carpano Antica Formula Vermouth**

1. Combine all of the ingredients in a mixing glass with ice. Stir until diluted to taste.
2. Strain the cocktail into a rocks glass, preferably over a large clear ice cube.
3. Express an orange peel (squeeze the peel to release the oils) over the cocktail and add the peel as a garnish on the rim of the glass.

GUILTY PLEASURES

SUNDAY VINYL
1803 16TH STREET, DENVER

When Frasca Hospitality Group opened Sunday Vinyl across from Tavernetta in 2019, the result was at once a jewel box of a wine bar, a niche spot to listen to an impressive array of vinyl, and an intimate spot to sip a terrific cocktail. Senior bartender Javaughn Marshall created this cocktail while pondering the whys and hows of the well-loved Amaretto Sour. "I've always wondered what it would look like to elevate this cocktail," he says. "And so, I set out on a mission to give the classic new life and bring a fall spin to it." This is a drink ideal for sipping when the leaves are changing colors or when the snow begins to fly.

GLASSWARE: Coupe glass
GARNISH: Grated cinnamon

- **1 oz. amaretto**
- **1 oz. brandy**
- **¾ oz. Cinnamon Demerara Syrup (see recipe)**
- **¾ oz. fresh lemon juice**
- **1 egg white**

1. Combine all of the ingredients in a shaker tin without ice and shake hard for 20 seconds.
2. Add ice to the shaker and shake again until the tin is cold.
3. Double-strain the cocktail into a coupe glass, and garnish with grated cinnamon.

CINNAMON DEMERARA SYRUP: Combine 250 grams demerara sugar and 250 grams water in a pot and boil until the sugar dissolves. Add 2 cinnamon sticks and simmer for 5 minutes or until the cinnamon flavor is incorporated. Cool, store, and refrigerate the syrup for up to 1 month.

GRACE TOMCZAK, MAKFAM

You wouldn't walk into MAKfam, an order-at-the-counter Cantonese-American restaurant in Denver's Baker neighborhood, and necessarily expect to discover cocktail brilliance. But with bar manager Grace Tomczak at the helm, that's just what you'll find. Her flagship recipe, the MSGin, is a bold, briney, in-your-face celebration of monosodium glutamate—and it pairs perfectly with the restaurant's big and bright flavors. "The other night I was in the back prepping and a girl came up and said, 'Are you the creator of MSGin? That is the best drink I've ever had in my life.' I was like, holy shit!" Tomczak—and cocktail culture—has certainly come a long way from her first bartending job in New York when the two most requested spirits were Absolut Peach and blue curaçao (sometimes mixed together).

Although Tomczak grew up on the East Coast, she went to school at CU Boulder before landing in New York City, and then Maui, before returning to Colorado in 2023. Tomczak, being the self-titled impatient, extrovert Sagittarius that she is, was restless and anxious to figure out the city. And then she found MAKfam owners (and fellow NYC-expats) Kenneth Wan and Doris Yuen. "The second I walked through the doors, I knew it was right," she says.

MAKfam's casual approach leads the staff to a lot of guest interaction and banter. "I come from resorts and fine dining so I'll admit I was apprehensive about counter service," Tomczak says. "But we're all fine-dining refugees here, getting down and dirty with our community. I've never had so many conversations [across the bar]." (MAKfam is the outgrowth of what started as the Meta Asian Kitchen pop-up in New York, morphed into a stall at Avanti Food & Beverage food hall in Denver, and is now a brick-and-mortar.)

Coinciding with her move to the Mile High City in 2023, Tomczak, a die-hard fan of a savory-leaning cocktail, has seen a welcome shift in drinking habits. "I've been making savory cocktails for seven years and no one cared. But now, she says, thanks to broadening culinary tastes and people looking for healthier ingredients, "people are shaking off the unknown and ordering something new." Tomczak, who lived and bartended in Queens, one of the most linguistically diverse boroughs in the world, pegs this multicultural immersion with shaping her cocktail tastes.

And it's not just Tomczak's approach to cocktails that's leaving an impression. MAKfam's come-one-come-all vibe contributes to the very welcome, trickle-down understanding that finely crafted beverages aren't the sole domain of high-end cocktail bars.

MSGIN

MAKFAM
39 WEST FIRST AVENUE, DENVER

When Grace Tomczak first met MAKfam owners Doris Yuen and Kenneth Wan, Yuen's first request was to put an MSG-forward cocktail on the menu. This fell in line with Tomczak's intention to push savory options, and she had recently moved from Maui, where celebrated Filipino chef Jojo Vasquez had taught her all about the magic of MSG (monosodium glutamate) as a flavor enhancer. The cocktail came together when Wan introduced Tomczak to brined Chinese plums and shaoxing, a Chinese cooking wine that's akin to boozy broth. It took some tinkering, but the final cocktail (and MAKfam signature) is big and bold. As Tomczak says, "This is not a cocktail for shrinking violets."

GLASSWARE: Coupe glass

- **MSGin Rim (see recipe), for the rim**
- **1½ oz. Barr Hill Gin**
- **1 oz. MSGin Brine (see recipe)**

1. Wet the rim of a coupe glass then dip the glass in MSGin Rim to give it a rim.
2. Combine the gin and brine in a cocktail shaker with ice and shake thoroughly.
3. Strain the cocktail into the rimmed coupe.

MSGin Rim: Combine 1 cup sugar, 1 cup MSG, 1 teaspoon salt, and the zest of 1 lemon in a bowl. Using gloved hands, massage the mixture to extract the oils from the lemon zest. Place a sieve over another bowl, add the mixture to the sieve, and tap to sift out the zest. (The point is to remove as much zest as possible.) Store the remaining mixture in an airtight container.

MSGin Brine: Combine 1 cup Enhanced Shaoxing (see recipe), ½ cup rice vinegar, and ½ cup Chinese plum brine in a glass container and stir to combine.

Enhanced Shaoxing: Combine 1 cup shaoxing wine and 2 teaspoons MSG in a glass container and stir until the MSG is dissolved.

HISS HISS BANG BANG

MAKFAM
39 WEST FIRST AVENUE, DENVER

Iced hibiscus tea was bar manager Grace Tomczak's go-to during her eight very hot, very humid summers in New York City. She would make giant batches of the tea, load up her water bottle, put on her headphones, and wander the city. Tomczak would often find herself in Chinatown, where she would buy a bag of fresh lychee from street vendors to peel and snack on. "That combo of hibiscus and lychee became the essence of summertime in a city," she says.

GLASSWARE: Collins glass
GARNISH: Mint leaves, lychee hard candy

- 1½ oz. vodka
- 1 oz. Lychee Syrup (see recipe)
- ¾ oz. fresh lemon juice
- ½ oz. blanc vermouth
- 8 drops rice vinegar
- 1 to 2 oz. hibiscus tea

1. Combine all of the ingredients, except for the tea, in a cocktail shaker with ice and shake to chill.
2. Strain the cocktail over fresh ice and top with tea.
3. Garnish with a cluster of mint leaves, a lychee hard candy, and serve with a crazy straw.

Lychee Syrup: Blend together 1 (15 oz.) can lychees, drained, 15 oz. sugar, 15 oz. water, and ½ teaspoon salt, ensuring that the sugar and salt are completely dissolved. Strain. Store the syrup in the refrigerator for 1 week.

HAUTE BOX

MAKFAM
39 WEST FIRST AVENUE, DENVER

One of bar manager Grace Tomczak's favorite places in New York City's Chinatown is the always bustling vegan Chinese restaurant called Buddha Bodai. Each time she dined, she'd order something new, including the cedar-braised bean curd skin. "The chewy, delicious tofu skin was stewed in a bright green, verdant broth that tasted like a forest I desperately wanted to be in," she says. That was years ago, but Tomczak has been chasing that woodsy flavor ever since. Enter the Haute Box, which is a white Negroni that trades bitterness for Rigi Alpine Liqueur's delicate cherry and botanical notes. Tomczak smokes the glass with cedar to bring it all back to that imaginary Chinatown forest she found herself lost in. For this recipe, you'll need a cedar wood grilling plank.

GLASSWARE: Rocks glass
GARNISH: 2 drops Mandarin Oil (see recipe)

- **1 oz. Martínez Lacuesta Extra Dry Vermouth**
- **1 oz. Kyrö Gin**
- **1 oz. Mount Rigi Swiss Aperitif**

1. Chill a rocks glass. Using a blowtorch, burn a spot on a cedar wood plank until it is smoking.

2. Place the chilled rocks glass upside down over the burnt spot, ensuring that smoke fills the glass.
3. Combine all of the ingredients in a mixing glass, add ice, and stir for 10 to 15 seconds.
4. Strain the cocktail over a big ice cube into the smoked glass.
5. Garnish by dotting the top of the ice cube with Mandarin Oil.

MANDARIN OIL: Take the peels from juiced mandarin halves, as needed, and lay them flat on a baking sheet lined with paper towels. Place another baking sheet on top, press down, and allow the peels to air dry for 24 to 48 hours, or until they have become dried out. Add the dried peels to a pot, then top with just enough safflower oil to cover them. Heat on medium until small bubbles begin to form on the bottom of the pot and pop while rising to the top. Remove the mixture from heat. Let the oil cool then strain and store in the refrigerator for up to 1 month.

THE YELLOW COCKTAIL

NOISETTE
3254 NAVAJO STREET #100, DENVER

When Tim Lu and Lillian Cho opened Noisette, their stunningly gorgeous ode to French cuisine in LoHi, in 2022, they wanted a cocktail menu that matched the level of cooking. Amanda Davenport, Noisette's bar manager, delivered. One such drink, The Yellow Cocktail, is a classic but it's often forgotten about. (If you're a fan of the Last Word, don't miss this variation.) Davenport was enticed by the cocktail's savory, herbal flavor profile and its vibrant color, and by including a touch of elderflower liqueur, she adds an elegant twist. Note: As Yellow Chartreuse becomes more difficult to source, génépy is a good substitute.

GLASSWARE: Coupe glass
GARNISH: Pansy

- **⅔ oz. Jones House Gin**
- **⅔ oz. Suze L'Originale**
- **⅔ oz. Yellow Chartreuse**
- **⅔ oz. fresh lemon juice**
- **¼ oz. elderflower liqueur**

1. Combine all of the ingredients in a cocktail shaker with ice and shake until chilled.
2. Strain the cocktail into a coupe and garnish with a pansy.

DUCK OLD FASHIONED

NOISETTE
3254 NAVAJO STREET #100, DENVER

Fat-washing a cocktail may give home bartenders pause, but it's just code for adding complexity to a beverage. "Fat-washed cocktails have a nice texture and a savory quality that is complementary to food," says bar manager Amanda Davenport. This cocktail came about as the LoHi restaurant always has a duck dish on the menu, and thus an excess of delicious duck fat.

GLASSWARE: Rocks glass
GARNISH: Orange twist

- **2½ oz. Duck Fat–Infused Bourbon (see recipe)**
- **Barspoon Demerara Simple Syrup (see recipe on page 18)**
- **2 dashes orange bitters**
- **2 dashes Angostura bitters**

1. Combine all of the ingredients in a mixing glass with ice and stir.
2. Strain the cocktail over a large ice cube into a rocks glass.
3. Garnish with an orange twist.

DUCK FAT–INFUSED BOURBON: Combine 1 (750 ml) bottle of Four Roses Bourbon and 4 oz. duck fat in a large, freezer-safe container and freeze for 12 to 24 hours. Remove the hardened fat off the top then strain through a coffee filter if necessary.

MISTAH BITTAH HAI

ADRIFT TIKI BAR
218 SOUTH BROADWAY, DENVER

The Mistah Bittah Hai came together somewhat early in Jacoby Morciglio's time at Adrift, a much-loved tiki bar that's been slinging drinks on South Broadway since 2012. The beverage manager's jumping off point was the Mr. Bali Hai cocktail from 1950s San Diego. "The original combines coffee and pineapple, but I wanted a more aperitif-style drink with Punt e Mes, which is one of my favorite things in the world," he says. Morciglio landed on grapefruit, with its slightly bitter backbone, and went with a funky Indonesian arrack and lightly smoky mezcal to complement the aperitif-and-coffee base of the drink. The final cocktail, like its inspiration, still holds the combination of tropical plus coffee near and dear.

GLASSWARE: 16-oz. glass
GARNISH: Mint, dehydrated grapefruit slice, smoking cinnamon stick

- 1¼ oz. Batavia-Arrack van Oosten
- ¾ oz. Punt e Mes
- ¾ oz. espadín mezcal
- ¾ oz. Cinnamon Syrup (see recipe)
- ¾ oz. fresh lime juice
- ¾ oz. fresh grapefruit juice
- Dash Angostura bitters
- Dash orange bitters

Cinnamon Syrup: Make a Simple Syrup (see recipe on page 18), adding cinnamon sticks, as needed, during the steeping and cooling phases and straining before use.

1. Combine all of the ingredients in a blender with 1 cup pebble or crushed ice, and flash blend by pulsing until chilled and aerated.
2. Pour the frozen cocktail into a 16-oz. glass and garnish with mint, a dehydrated grapefruit slice, and a smoking cinnamon stick.

MAI TAI

ADRIFT TIKI BAR
218 SOUTH BROADWAY, DENVER

The Mai Tai is a quintessential tropical drink from Trader Vic's in the 1940s. This drink has seen more scrutiny, gossip, and bastardization than almost any other cocktail in history, says beverage manager Jacoby Morciglio. "Our Mai Tai, engineered by bartender Vince Polizzi, is an homage to the OG in spirit choice and balance," Morciglio explains. Adrift includes some Guyanese 151 rum like Trader Vic's, along with a bold and flavorful Jamaican rum blend. The tiki bar also makes some minor adjustments, such as including a pinch of salt to enhance flavor and a rich orgeat to achieve balance without relying on rock candy syrup. These subs control the dilution a bit more while also keeping a whisper of almond.

GLASSWARE: Mai tai glass
GARNISH: Mint, spent lime shell, edible orchid

- **1 oz. fresh lime juice**
- **¾ oz. Worthy Park 109 Jamaica Rum**
- **¾ oz. Smith & Cross Jamaica Rum**
- **¾ oz. orgeat**
- **⅓ oz. Hamilton Petite Shrubb**
- **¼ oz. Hamilton 151 Overproof Demerara Rum**
- **Pinch salt**

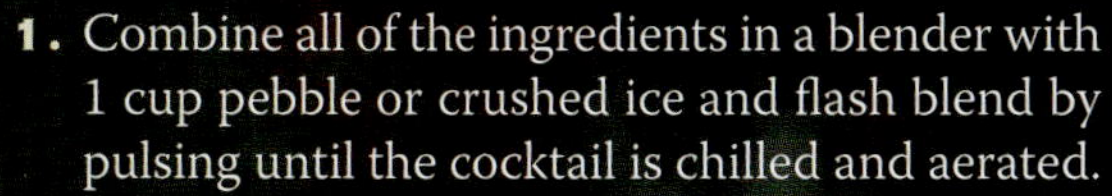

1. Combine all of the ingredients in a blender with 1 cup pebble or crushed ice and flash blend by pulsing until the cocktail is chilled and aerated.
2. Pour the frozen cocktail into a mai tai glass and garnish with mint, a spent lime shell, and an edible orchid.

STUART WEAVER, LADY JANE AND TWO MOONS MUSIC HALL

If you can't find Stuart Weaver, partner and general manager of LoHi cocktail bar Lady Jane's, slinging drinks behind the swanky, mid-century-modern bar, he's almost certainly out exploring Colorado's mountains. The Texas native might be temporarily out of cell range, but he'll be back.

Weaver has only been in Denver for five years—he moved from Washington, DC, after spending a decade working on the financial side of the hospitality industry—but, boy, has he made a mark. Lady Jane, which opened in LoHi in 2018 and is a sister spot to Hudson Hill, The Wild, and Two Moons, is currently one of the most exciting cocktail bars in town.

"We're at the forefront," says Weaver. "I love pushing the boundaries with new techniques and new flavors." When he landed at Lady Jane, shortly before the pandemic, he took over the program and focused on super-approachable but extremely well-made cocktails. That gave him time to learn about Denver's (and, specifically, LoHi's) bar crowd. "I thought approachability was what people wanted," he continues. "But the weirder, more esoteric the cocktail, the more popular it became. People want the weird stuff, they want interesting flavors and techniques, and drinks that are thought-provoking."

Although Lady Jane's cocktails take full advantage of an extensive backbar, the staff's favorite spirits to work with tend to be mezcal, gin, and rum. Weaver, for one, is obsessed with Scotch and amaro. "We have fifty to sixty amari on the backbar, and we kind of find our way to sneak it into everything," he says. "I wouldn't say we're an amari bar at all, but people keep getting them, drinking them, and asking questions about them."

Weaver oversees a staff of twelve and everyone works full time. "The bar program is way too big and we're constantly changing the menu and rolling out new cocktails," Weaver says. "Everyone has a cocktail on the menu so they have ownership of the space."

Weaver really believes in nurturing the career bartender. Of course there are times and places for the I-need-some-cash side gig, but he thinks those who are most dedicated to the craft are the ones giving the most back to the scene. "Look at those who are succeeding the most," he says, "They—Yacht Club, Death & Co, Williams & Graham—they are the ones making this industry their life."

CON TODO

LADY JANE
2021 WEST 32ND AVENUE, DENVER

When creating cocktails, food is a big inspiration for Lady Jane bartender Danny Garcia. "Going to the taquería with my Mexican grandfather was one of the ways we connected," he says. "I was the only one in my family interested in going with him to get menudo on Saturday mornings or for tacos de lengua, cabeza, and tripa." The flavors of tacos al pastor resonated with Garcia, and he thought they could translate to a cocktail. The name of the drink comes from the most important question you get from a taquero ("taco maker") when ordering tacos: "¿Con todo?" ("With everything?"), meaning, cilantro, onion, and salsa.

GLASSWARE: Double rocks glass
GARNISH: Wrapped fresh pineapple moon

- **Cilantro-Lime Salt (see recipe), for the rim**
- **1½ oz. Corn Tortilla–Infused Mezcal (see recipe)**
- **1 oz. Al Pastor Syrup (see recipe)**
- **¾ oz. fresh lime juice**
- **½ oz. pineapple juice**
- **1 pipette Saline Solution (see recipe on page 19)**

1. Rim a double rocks glass with Cilantro-Lime Salt.
2. Combine the remaining ingredients in a cocktail shaker with ice and shake until cold.
3. Fine-strain the cocktail over a big ice cube into the rimmed glass.
4. Garnish by wrapping a fresh pineapple half-moon on the inside of the glass.

Cilantro-Lime Salt: Combine ½ bunch cilantro, washed and drained, the zest of 3 limes, and 2 cups Diamond Kosher Salt in a blender and blend to the point where there are no more large pieces of cilantro or lime. The end product should look like bright green, slightly moist sand. Transfer the mixture to a sheet tray lined with parchment paper and bake at 170°F for 30 to 40 minutes, occasionally mixing it with a fork so it does not clump up. Allow the mixture to cool, fluff it with a fork, and store refrigerated for up to 1 month.

Corn Tortilla–Infused Mezcal: Toast 3 corn tortillas in a pan over medium heat. Toast on both sides until there are brown spots and the tortillas are crispy. Combine the toasted tortillas in a large bowl with 1 (750 ml) bottle of Rey Campero Espadín Mezcal, cover, and let the infusion sit at room temperature for 24 hours. Rebottle and store indefinitely.

Al Pastor Syrup: In a pot over low heat, combine 16 grams guajillo chile, destemmed and deseeded; 14 grams California chiles, destemmed and deseeded; 10 grams achiote or annatto seed; 10 grams cinnamon; 4 grams nutmeg; 4 grams chiles de arbol, destemmed; and 0.5 gram oregano. Add 400 grams demerara sugar, 400 grams water, 22.5 grams Saline Solution (see recipe on page 19), and 10 grams apple cider vinegar, and increase the heat to medium. Stir until the sugar is dissolved. Remove the syrup from heat and let it sit for 24 hours. Strain and refrigerate for up to 2 weeks.

EXPEDITIONS

LADY JANE
2021 WEST 32ND AVENUE, DENVER

This is a classic Daiquiri riff, and more specifically, a split-base (two spirits are used for the drink's foundation) play on a Gold Rush. The cocktail is light and refreshing with an unctuous, cinnamon character coming from the amburana cachaça, which is a Brazilian rum made from sugarcane juice. "The maple and mole bitters give the drink a wintry spice that plays well with the rye and the cachaça," general manager Stuart Weaver says.

GLASSWARE: **Tiki glass**
GARNISH: **Lime wedge**

- **Mole Mixture (see recipe), for the rim**
- **¾ oz. Sazerac Rye**
- **¾ oz. Avuá Cachaça Amburana**
- **¾ oz. Maple Syrup (see recipe)**
- **¾ oz. fresh lime juice**
- **2 dashes Bittermens Xocolatl Mole Bitters**

1. Combine all of the ingredients in a cocktail shaker with ice and shake until cold.
2. Dip half the rim of a tiki glass into the Mole Mixture to give the glass a rim.
3. Double-strain the cocktail over a large ice cube into the glass.
4. Etch a lime wedge by scoring the skin of a lime with a four-point zester, then add the wedge as a garnish.

Mole Mixture: Combine equal parts dried guajillo chile, stem and seeds removed; dried pasilla chile, stem and seeds removed; dried morita chile, stem and seeds removed; coriander seeds, toasted; lime zest; and salt in a blender and pulverize. Sift the mole through a fine-mesh strainer. Place any remaining large pieces back in the blender and repeat the process until there are no large pieces. Store the mole indefinitely in a glass container.

Maple Syrup: Combine maple syrup and water at a 3:1 ratio. Stir to incorporate. Store in a glass container for three months.

LAVA MAMA

LADY JANE
2021 WEST 32ND AVENUE, DENVER

The original idea behind this cocktail was to riff on the Naked & Famous, but after general manager Stuart Weaver took a trip to Hawaii, he decided to give the cocktail some Hawaiian influence. "I named the cocktail after Pele, the Hawaiian volcano deity, an elemental force and the creator of those volcanic landscapes," he says. According to tradition, Pele is embodied by the lava and natural forces associated with volcanic eruptions.

GLASSWARE: Nick & Nora glass

GARNISH: Aperol-Soaked Dehydrated Pineapple Flower (see recipe)

- ¾ oz. Kuleana Rum Works Huihui
- ¾ oz. Madre Mezcal Espadín
- ½ oz. Pineapple-and-Lime-Infused Aperol (see recipe)
- ½ oz. Cocchi Americano
- ¼ oz. Yellow Chartreuse
- ¼ oz. Rhine Hall Mango Eau de Vie

1. Chill a Nick & Nora glass. Combine all of the ingredients in a mixing glass with ice and stir.
2. Strain the cocktail into the chilled Nick & Nora.

Pineapple-and-Lime-Infused Aperol: Peel 1 pineapple, reserving the skins, then slice it into wheels as thinly as possible. Combine the pineapple skins, pineapple wheels, and 30 grams lime peel with 1 (1 liter) bottle of Aperol in a bowl, cover, and let the mixture sit at room temperature for 24 hours. Strain, reserving the pineapple wheels, and rebottle.

Aperol-Soaked Dehydrated Pineapple Flower: Place the reserved pineapple wheels from the Pineapple-and-Lime-Infused Aperol recipe in a dehydrator at 135°F for 24 hours.

EASY LOVER

TWO MOONS MUSIC HALL
2944 LARIMER STREET, DENVER

What's fun about Two Moons is that it's a concert venue and a cocktail bar all rolled into one. While bar wiz (and partner) Stuart Weaver carefully designed the cocktails, he did so with speed in mind. "Two Moons is set up to move," says owner Jake Soffes. "Stuart's cocktails are designed to be drinkable and produced really quickly." One such example of this high-concept, low-effort affair is the wild Easy Lover. With the first sip comes mango and then a surprising hint of raspberry, but the mid-palate is all cacao and it finishes with a lingering curry flavor.

GLASSWARE: Footed highball glass
GARNISH: Mint bouquet

- 1½ oz. Tequila Cazadores Blanco
- ¾ oz. fresh lime juice
- ½ oz. Giffard White Crème de Cacao
- ½ oz. Fruitful Mixology Mango Liqueur
- Barspoon Curry Tincture (see recipe)
- Barspoon Clear Creek Raspberry Brandy

1. Combine all of the ingredients in a cocktail shaker with only one or two pieces of ice and shake until the ice melts. (This is called a whip shake and it creates a frothy texture.)
2. Pour the cocktail into a footed highball and garnish with a cluster of mint leaves and a long straw.

Curry Tincture: Combine 300 ml Epic Vodka Classic, 20 grams Madras curry powder, and 4 grams dried turmeric in a bowl, cover, and let the mixture sit at room temperature for 24 hours. Strain, making sure to press the curry powder down to maximize the yield. Store the tincture in a glass container at room temperature for up to 3 months.

8 AM

HUDSON HILL
619 EAST 13TH AVENUE, DENVER

Located in the heart of Capitol Hill, Hudson Hill is half coffee shop, half craft cocktail bar. When it first opened in 2016, it was the first of its kind in Denver and it built a following quickly. The 8 AM was on the opening menu, and it's an amalgamation of all things boozy and bitter. Fresh espresso, amaro, and bourbon work together seamlessly to create what is essentially a simple, even-parts cocktail, with a twist of lemon as an homage to the antiquated espresso shot garnish. Though it drinks as an Espresso Martini, the team very quickly realized this cocktail was a perfect breakfast beverage, hence the name 8 AM.

GLASSWARE: Rocks glass
GARNISH: Lemon twist

- **1½ oz. fresh espresso**
- **1 oz. bourbon**
- **1 oz. Paolucci Amaro CioCiaro**

1. Combine all of the ingredients in a cocktail shaker and add ice.
2. Shake vigorously and strain the cocktail into a rocks glass over fresh ice.
3. Garnish with a lemon twist.

THE GREEN HOUR

HUDSON HILL
619 EAST 13TH AVENUE, DENVER

One afternoon, Hudson Hill's bar manager, Daniela Solano, came to work with a huge smile on her face, simply stating, "I have something really weird and very good in mind." The ensuing tiki-themed Margarita was Solano's first cocktail that made it on the menu, and it was the bestselling drink for six months. The Green Hour may have rotated off the cocktail list nearly a decade ago, but it's still requested to this day.

GLASSWARE: Coupe glass
GARNISH: Grated nutmeg

- **1½ oz. blanco tequila**
- **¾ oz. Cinnamon Simple Syrup (see recipe)**
- **¾ oz. cream of coconut**
- **½ oz. fresh lime juice**
- **½ oz. triple sec**
- **¼ oz. crème de menthe**

1. Combine all of the ingredients in a cocktail shaker with ice and shake vigorously.
2. Fine-strain the cocktail over ice into a coupe and garnish with freshly grated nutmeg.

CINNAMON SIMPLE SYRUP: In a small pan over medium-low heat, toast 8 cinnamon sticks until fragrant. Add 1 cup hot water and 1 cup sugar and bring the mixture to a low boil. Remove from heat and allow the syrup to cool. Strain.

WILD FASHION

THE WILD
1600 WYNKOOP STREET, SUITE 100, DENVER

Despite sitting across the street from Union Station, The Wild feels like a secret. This coffee shop by day, bar by night is set back from the street just enough that you might walk right on by. But find it and you've stumbled on a treasure. (Owner Jake Soffes chose the name because of how the space feels separate from reality, just like the famous children's story *Where the Wild Things Are*.) A house favorite, the Wild Fashion was designed to be an all-season cocktail: the light-on-the-palate Old Fashioned tracks just as well on a summer patio as it does watching snow fall. The inspiration behind creating the orange cardamom oleo came from one of Soffes' favorite pastries, a simple morning bun from Hearth Bakery on Lawrence Street.

GLASSWARE: Double rocks glass

GARNISH: Lemon twist

- **1½ oz. Old Overholt Straight Rye Whiskey**
- **¾ oz. manzanilla sherry**
- **½ oz. Orange Cardamom Oleo (see recipe)**
- **3 dashes Peychaud's bitters**

1. Combine all of the ingredients in a mixing glass and stir.
2. Pour the cocktail over a large ice cube into a double rocks glass and garnish with a lemon twist.

Orange Cardamom Oleo: Peel 2 oranges and place the peels in a sealable container, then lightly muddle the peels. Add 1 cup white sugar, cover the container, and let it sit overnight at room temperature. Add 4 to 5 cinnamon sticks and 4 tablespoons cardamom seeds to a pot over medium heat, stirring frequently until the spices become aromatic. Add 1 cup hot water and bring the mixture to a light boil. Add the sugar–orange peel mixture, return the pot to a boil, and stir until the sugar has dissolved. Remove the oleo from heat and let it cool. Fine-strain and store the oleo in the refrigerator for up to 2 weeks.

EASY SAILOR

THE WILD
1600 WYNKOOP STREET, SUITE 100, DENVER

This gin Martini variant—consider it an update to the Martinez—is a great introduction to stirred cocktails. It's smooth, approachable, and easily made from products found on the shelf of any liquor store. The blend of vermouths and amaro delivers excellent cocoa and vanilla notes and the navy-strength gin provides extra kick. When drinking a simple but luxurious Easy Sailor, it's best to envision oneself on a sailboat off the coast of Italy.

GLASSWARE: Nick & Nora glass
GARNISH: Lemon peel

- 1¼ oz. Jones House Gin
- ½ oz. Dolin Blanc Vermouth
- ½ oz. Cocchi Storico Vermouth di Torino
- ¼ oz. navy-strength gin
- ¼ oz. Amaro Montenegro
- 2 dashes orange bitters

1. Combine all of the ingredients in a mixing glass and stir.
2. Pour the cocktail into a Nick & Nora and garnish with a lemon peel.

BOMBA ROSA

THE WILD
1600 WYNKOOP STREET, SUITE 100, DENVER

The Bomba Rosa is the essence of spring in a glass. A house-made syrup is used as the backbone of the cocktail and provides a juicy floral flavor that can't be beat. Pink peppercorn–infused gin adds depth and elevates the character of the drink in a bright and austere manner. "I always like to have at least one bright pink cocktail on our menu," says general manager and coffee director Anders Lehto. "They're always the most fun to conceptualize."

GLASSWARE: Large coupe glass
GARNISH: Ground pink peppercorns

- **2 oz. Pink Peppercorn–Infused Gin (see recipe)**
- **¾ oz. aquafaba**
- **¾ oz. fresh lemon juice**
- **¾ oz. Strawberry-Rose Syrup (see recipe)**
- **3 dashes Peychaud's bitters**

1. Combine all of the ingredients in a cocktail shaker and dry-shake without ice.
2. Add ice and shake again.
3. Double-strain the cocktail into a large coupe.
4. Garnish with ground pink peppercorns.

Pink Peppercorn-Infused Gin: Add 45 grams pink peppercorns to 1 (1 liter) bottle of Jones House Gin. Set the gin aside to infuse at room temperature for at least 12 hours before straining.

Strawberry-Rose Syrup: Make Simple Syrup (see recipe on page 18), adding 1 tablespoon Tulsi Sweet Rose Tea as the syrup is simmering, and simmer for 5 minutes. Blend ½ cup strawberries. Strain the tea syrup, then add it to the blender with the strawberries and blend until smooth. Strain and refrigerate the syrup for up to 1 month.

Chris Donato and Jeff Yeatman

CHRIS DONATO AND JEFF YEATMAN, CHAMPAGNE TIGER

Sometimes the party must go on. That's the lesson of the futuristic, Jetsons-esque building that houses Champagne Tiger. Originally built as Tom's Diner in the 1960s, the Colfax Avenue structure has been praised for its futuristic architecture, but it was nearly bulldozed until interested citizens worked tirelessly to land it on the National Registry of Historic Places.

Co-owners Chris Donato and husband Jeff Yeatman live just two blocks away from the iconic building, and after three years of hosting Champagne Tiger pop-ups and drag brunches around the city, Donato knew there was no better place to house his larger-than-life concept. In the spring of 2024, the vibrant American-diner-meets-French-brasserie flung open its doors with a fitting tagline of "celebrate everyday."

"The mission of Champagne Tiger," says Donato, who is both owner and general manager, "is to curate joy." Donato, who spent more than a decade in fine dining with the Frasca Hospitality Group, knows all the touch points of tip-top service and hospitality, and he wanted to democratize it. "This is all about playful experiences that have no pretense, it's bougie high-low." On that note, the space is decidedly mid-century modern with a menu peddling ice-cold Champagne and freshly shucked Wellfleet oysters, right alongside stacked burgers with fries and plates of roasted chicken. The cocktails are equally fun and smile-inducing, with names like Caddy Issues, Gold Trans-Am, and Striptease Falcon.

At Champagne Tiger, Donato underscores that all walks of life are welcomed and celebrated. And between the drag brunches, Piano & Pasta Wednesdays, and the neighborhood regulars, Champagne Tiger draws a boisterous crowd.

PRINCETONIAN

CHAMPAGNE TIGER
601 EAST COLFAX AVENUE, DENVER

This French bistro-meets-American diner is the ultimate mish-mash celebration of all things and all people. As bartender Jon Coklyat was dreaming up cocktails, he saw the opportunity to showcase his home state of New Jersey, the diner capital of the country. Interestingly enough, during the pandemic, the most googled cocktail in New Jersey was . . . the Piña Colada. "I chose to create an elevated Piña Colada riff using some of my favorite ingredients," Coklyat says. In the Princetonian, hibiscus provides bright and tart notes while baking spice and raisin come from a combo of allspice dram and sherry.

GLASSWARE: Double rocks glass
GARNISH: Hibiscus flowers on top of a large ice cube

- 1½ oz. Hibiscus-Infused Vodka (see recipe)
- 1 oz. pineapple juice
- ¾ oz. organic coconut water
- ½ oz. fresh lime juice
- ½ oz. Lustau Pedro Ximénez San Emilio
- ¼ oz. Rich Simple Syrup (see recipe on page 18)
- Barspoon St. Elizabeth Allspice Dram
- 1 oz. whole milk

1. Combine all of the ingredients, except for the milk, in a mixing glass and stir.
2. Pour the milk into a separate container.
3. Slowly pour the cocktail into the milk and allow the drink to curdle.
4. Run the mixture through a coffee filter.
5. Strain the cocktail into a double rocks glass over a large ice cube and garnish with hibiscus flowers.

Hibiscus-Infused Vodka: In a large mason jar, combine 1 liter vodka, 20 grams dried hibiscus, 15 grams cinnamon sticks, 10 grams orange peel, and 10 whole cloves, stir, and let the infusion rest for at least 24 hours. Agitate it, then strain the vodka through a fine-mesh strainer into a new large mason jar. Refrigerate for up to 3 months.

STRIPTEASE FALCON

CHAMPAGNE TIGER
601 EAST COLFAX AVENUE, DENVER

This cocktail is inspired by the modern classic Porn Star Martini, a drink that bartender Emily Horn has always considered a fun, cheeky option that is easy to enjoy. "The energy I wanted to bring to the menu and to our space at Champagne Tiger is a playful and unexpected one, so this seemed like the perfect addition," Horn says. "The Striptease Falcon is meant to be a flirtatious drink that evokes this ethos."

GLASSWARE: Martini glass
GARNISH: Grated cinnamon

- **1 oz. vodka**
- **¾ oz. fresh lemon juice**
- **½ oz. Norden Aquavit**
- **½ oz. Giffard Crème de Fruits de la Passion**
- **¼ oz. vanilla syrup**
- **1 teaspoon cinnamon syrup**
- **½ oz. egg white**

1. Combine all of the ingredients in a cocktail shaker and dry-shake without ice.
2. Open the tins, add ice, and shake vigorously.
3. Double-strain the cocktail into a martini glass and grate cinnamon over top.

CAROLINE CLARK, HEY KIDDO AND OK YEAH

When Hey Kiddo opened on the top floor of the Asher Hotel in Denver's Berkeley neighborhood in January 2023, it was (at the time) the fifth concept from James Beard Award–winning restaurateur Kelly Whitaker and the Id Est Hospitality group. It cooks up a "good and fun" menu that is bold, fusion-y, and threaded through with Korean flavors and technique. (The seed for the restaurant grew out of pop-up collabs between Whitaker and San Francisco chef Deuki Hong, who is the author of *Koreatown* and *Koreaworld*).

The cocktails are equally bold, sometimes bordering on confounding (at least on paper), which means bartenders are always ready to answer questions. One might ask, "Why is lacto-fermented tomato water in my cocktail?" (Try it!)

Hey Kiddo also has a secret, which is only revealed after one weaves, somewhat awkwardly, through the service station at the back of the restaurant. This is Ok Yeah, a fifteen-seat, of-the-moment cocktail bar. There's no set menu; instead a chat with the bartender yields a cocktail customized to your tastes. If that sounds hoity-toity, it is, in fact, very low-key and fun. The bar is helmed by true creatives and cocktail historians who can translate your basic drinking preferences into mind-blowingly good cocktails.

Ok Yeah also serves another purpose: It's one of the many ways Hey Kiddo repurposes its food waste. Here, what might be discarded at one place gets another chance. "It's about full utilization," says Caroline Clark, director of beverage and hospitality for all of the Id Est concepts (Basta, Wolf's Tailor, Brutø, Dry Storage, Hey Kiddo, and Ok Yeah). "We can make sense of trim [the pieces usually discarded] and give it another life in food and beverage."

For example, something like beef tallow can be used to fat-wash cocktails, and kimchi water can find its way into a savory cocktail. "OK Yeah is about smaller volume so we have the luxury of using things we have less of," says Clark, who in 2023 won the Michelin Guide's Colorado Exceptional Cocktail Award. Hey Kiddo, Ok Yeah, and all of the Id Est restaurants share the same ethos: exquisite food and drink with an eye on zero waste.

Hey Kiddo

FANTÔMAS

HEY KIDDO
4337 TENNYSON STREET, DENVER

At its core, Fantômas is an accessible and easy-to-read cocktail that relies on high-quality ingredients that are also exciting to bar enthusiasts. In addition, bartenders Davey Anderson and Mitchell Armstrong wanted Fantômas to be a drink that catches the eye, where guests see it walk past them on a tray and say, "What's that? I want one of those!" The name is a reference to an early twentieth-century fictional spy in French pop culture. He is often referred to as inspiration for more modern stealthy characters such as the Pink Panther and even Batman. The cocktail's bright blue hue invokes the image of the blue-masked Fantômas from his character in films, with the drink itself playing as a subtle nod to his skills in deception and subterfuge.

GLASSWARE: Collins glass
GARNISH: Orange slice

- 1 oz. vodka
- 1 oz. Kina L'Aero d'Or
- ¾ oz. fresh lemon juice
- ½ oz. egg white
- ½ oz. Lemongrass Simple Syrup (see recipe)
- ¼ oz. blue curaçao
- Haykin Family Cider Golden Russet, to top

1. Combine all of the ingredients, except for the cider, in a cocktail shaker with ice and shake.
2. Strain and shake again, without ice.
3. Double-strain the cocktail into a collins glass and top with cider. Garnish with an orange slice.

Lemongrass Simple Syrup: Make Simple Syrup (see recipe on page 18), adding 2 stalks lemongrass, bruised and sliced into ½ inch pieces, to the saucepan while the syrup is cooking. Allow the syrup to cool and strain.

PEACEWALKER

HEY KIDDO
4337 TENNYSON STREET, DENVER

This cocktail is inspired by the Floradora, a bright pink classic. The original was named after a wildly successful Edwardian play that takes place on a fictional island in the South Pacific. As the story goes, a wealthy British aristocrat, Cyrus W. Gilfain, steals a perfume recipe made from the Floradora flower essence and intrigue ensues. In beverage form, the flavor combo of lemon, ginger, and raspberry is light, fruity, and slightly sweet. Bartender Davey Anderson's riff is named after Hey Kiddo's cheery mascot, the sneakered Peacewalker (envision a two-fingered peace sign with feet). Anderson played with less common spirits to add complexity: Singani 63 is a fascinatingly bright Bolivian brandy; Empirical Symphony 6 is an uncategorized distillate that explores the fragrant leaves of mandarin, lemon, coffee, black currant, and fig. This is certainly a recipe for which Gilfain would commit a crime in modern times.

GLASSWARE: Rocks glass
GARNISH: Lemon wheel

- **1½ oz. Singani 63**
- **¾ oz. fresh lemon juice**
- **½ oz. Empirical Symphony 6**
- **½ oz. Raspberry Syrup (see recipe)**
- **½ oz. Ginger Syrup (see recipe)**
- **2 oz. soda water, to top**

1. Combine all of the ingredients, except for the soda water, in a cocktail shaker with ice and shake.
2. Double-strain the cocktail over a large ice cube, top with soda water, and garnish with a lemon wheel.

RASPBERRY SYRUP: Combine 500 grams raspberries, 500 grams sugar, 500 grams water, and 5 grams citric acid in a saucepan and bring the mixture to a boil. Reduce to a simmer and cover, stirring occasionally, for 2 hours. Store refrigerated for up to 2 weeks.

GINGER SYRUP: Peel fresh ginger, as needed, chop it into 1-inch chunks, then juice and strain it through a chinois until you have 500 ml. In a blender, add the ginger juice and blend at a low setting with the lid off. Slowly pour in 1,000 grams white sugar. Blend, covered, at a medium speed until the sugar is dissolved. Store refrigerated for up to 2 weeks.

GREEN TOMATO GIMLET

THE WOLF'S TAILOR
4058 TEJON STREET, DENVER

In 2023, the kitchen and bar teams at The Wolf's Tailor challenged themselves to source as close to one hundred percent Colorado ingredients as possible. The menu launched in early spring, when fresh produce ingredients were still quite limited but the warming weather had many craving refreshing flavor profiles. As citrus is not locally available, this cocktail came out of bartender Robert Clark's efforts to reimagine citrus-driven cocktails without the use of it directly. Green tomato was selected as an adjacent to citric acid's structure. The Gimlet was designed as a pairing to The Wolf's Tailor's famous wood-fired piada bread, which at the time was being served with a house herb butter. Clark selected a botanical gin that spoke to the early sprouting spring herbs available.

GLASSWARE: Nick & Nora glass
GARNISH: Viola flowers

- **2 oz. Mythology Foragers Botanical Gin**
- **1 oz. Green Tomato-Mint Syrup (see recipe)**

1. Combine the gin and syrup in a cocktail shaker tin with ice and shake.
2. Double-strain the cocktail into a Nick & Nora glass.
3. Garnish with viola flowers.

GREEN TOMATO-MINT SYRUP: Add 400 grams fine-strained green tomato juice to a blender and blend on low. Slowly add 300 grams sugar, 34 grams citric acid, 8 grams malic acid, 15 grams fresh mint leaves, and 1 to 2 drops chlorophyll. Blend on high until the sugar is dissolved. Fine-strain and store the syrup in an airtight container.

DOCKSIDE

THE WOLF'S TAILOR
4058 TEJON STREET, DENVER

In tandem with The Wolf's Tailor's effort to prioritize exclusively local and seasonal bar components, the restaurant uses preserved shrubs from its rich pantry of house-made vinegars to bring acid to complex Sour-style cocktails. By choosing Leopold Bros' sour lime cordial, Atōst Roots Aperitif, and gin from biodynamical producer CapRock for this cocktail, bartender Lee Clark showcases Colorado distilleries producing unconventional spirits and cordials. Together, the spirits blend for a savory and refreshing sip. The resulting drink also has a distinct salinity to it, something that reminded us of enjoying a beverage by the water. Note: Atōst has recently moved its operations to California.

GLASSWARE: Coupe glass

- **1 oz. CapRock Organic Gin**
- **½ oz. Leopold Bros Sour Lime Cordial**
- **½ oz. Atōst California Aperitif**
- **½ oz. Leopold Bros Maraschino Cherry Liqueur**
- **½ oz. Russian Sage Balsamic Shrub (see recipe)**

1. Combine all of the ingredients in a cocktail shaker with ice and shake.
2. Strain the cocktail into a coupe.

Russian Sage Balsamic Shrub: Combine 300 grams Russian sage and 1 gallon white balsamic vinegar in a large airtight container and steep in a cool, dark place for at least 2 weeks. Strain and store in glass for up to 3 months.

HOWLING WOLF

THE WOLF'S TAILOR
4058 TEJON STREET, DENVER

At the end of the tasting menu in 2023, The Wolf's Tailor offered guests a beverage option: wind down with warm tea or turn up with the Howling Wolf, an Irish Coffee riff. The cocktail was inspired by the restaurant's proprietary blend of Devoción Coffee and celebrates Colorado distilleries by blending together cold brew with a locally distilled aged rum and dry curaçao. It sips with a rich molasses character balanced with orange, toffee, and chocolate notes. Bartender Jonnie Long recommends whipping your own cream, and ensures this cocktail will keep you going long after dinner has ended.

GLASSWARE: Stemmed cordial glass
GARNISH: Whipped cream, grated coffee bean

- **1 oz. cold brew**
- **¾ oz. Ironton Barrel Aged Rum**
- **¼ oz. Golden Moon Dry Curaçao**
- **¼ oz. cane syrup**
- **1 teaspoon Smith & Cross Jamaica Rum**

1. Combine all of the ingredients in a shaker tin with ice and shake vigorously until cold.
2. Double-strain the cocktail into a stemmed cordial glass.
3. Garnish with whipped cream and grate a coffee bean over the top.

NO. 3

BRUTØ
1801 BLAKE STREET, DENVER

Brutø prides itself on its commitment to brutalism, a raw, utilitarian movement that eschews aesthetics in favor of ethics. The kitchen and bar teams work in tandem, exploring ingredients in their various natural states. This fan-favorite cocktail showcases bartender Brandy Polack's deep adoration for Colorado's tomato season. Along with seasonality, sustainability is essential to Brutø, and lacto-fermentation is a way to both preserve and alter the flavor profile of tomatoes. This brine initially made its way to the bar from cross-utilization practices in Brutø's efforts to limit waste. Pairing the salinity of the tomato brine with the complex flavors of the tomato jam creates a savory Margarita or Bloody Maria riff unlike any you've tasted before.

GLASSWARE: Rocks glass

GARNISH: Halved cherry tomato on a pick, salt, pepper

- **1 oz. Arette Blanco Tequila**
- **¾ oz. Lacto-Fermented Tomato Water (see recipe)**
- **¾ oz. fresh lime juice**
- **½ oz. agave nectar**
- **½ oz. Cocchi Americano**
- **½ oz. Banhez Mezcal**
- **Barspoon Tomato Jam (see recipe)**

1. Combine all of the ingredients in a cocktail shaker with ice and shake.

2. Fine-strain the cocktail into a rocks glass.
3. Garnish with a halved cherry tomato on a pick, a shake of salt, and a shake of pepper.

Lacto-Fermented Tomato Water: Using a kitchen scale, weigh 2 heirloom tomatoes. Measure out 3% of the tomato weight in salt. (Example: 200 grams tomatoes x 3% = 6 grams salt.) Muddle salt and tomatoes together in a container. Leave the container covered at room temperature for 5 days. Stir and muddle daily. Strain the tomato water through a fine-mesh strainer or chinois, and store it in the refrigerator for up to 2 weeks.

Tomato Jam: Combine 1,169 grams tomato, seeds removed, chopped; 1,169 grams sugar; 50 grams cinnamon sticks; 50 grams black peppercorns; 20 grams ginger, peeled and grated; the zest and juice of 2 lemons; and 60 grams balsamic vinegar in a pot and heat for 30 minutes over low-medium heat (do not boil). Strain (without pressing the solids), and then return the solids to the pot over low heat. Reduce the solids to a thick jam texture. Remove the cinnamon sticks and store in the refrigerator for up to one month.

ALBATROSS

COOPER LOUNGE
1701 WYNKOOP STREET, DENVER

According to Cooper Lounge bartender Hunter Byrne, this cocktail is named after the large oceanic bird (or possibly the famous Coleridge poem "The Rime of the Ancient Mariner") that's often associated with burden and regret. Byrne choose chamomile for its medicinal qualities said to aid in sleeplessness and anxiety—which are also, probably not coincidentally, symptoms of regret. The drink itself looks like a fall–early winter ocean sky at dawn or sunset.

GLASSWARE: **Coupe glass**
GARNISH: **Gin spritz, dried chamomile flowers**

- **6 blueberries, muddled**
- **1½ oz. Chamomile-Infused Gin (see recipe)**
- **¾ oz. fresh lemon juice**
- **¾ oz. Simple Syrup (see recipe on page 18)**
- **¾ oz. egg white**
- **½ oz. génépy**

1. Combine all of the ingredients in a cocktail shaker without ice and dry-shake to froth the egg white.
2. Add ice and shake again.
3. Double-strain the cocktail into a coupe.
4. Spritz with gin and garnish with chamomile flowers.

Chamomile-Infused Gin: Combine 1 (750 ml) bottle of Barr Hill Gin and ⅓ cup chamomile flowers, dried or fresh, and let the infusion stand for 15 minutes. Strain and rebottle.

KOGANI NO MORI

COOPER LOUNGE
1701 WYNKOOP STREET, DENVER

K*ogani no Mori*, which translates to "Golden Forest" in Japanese, is an alpine-style White Manhattan. It drinks dry and light with vegetal, starchy notes from the sherry and Japanese rice whiskey. The génépy brings forth pine and clean sugar, and a bit of vanilla lactic provides rounded warm undertones. Grapefruit bitters and rosemary tincture balance and tie the cocktail together.

GLASSWARE: Nick & Nora glass
GARNISH: Rosemary sprig

- **1½ oz. Kikori Rice Whiskey**
- **¾ oz. génépy**
- **½ oz. fino sherry**
- **Barspoon Vanilla Syrup (see recipe)**
- **2 dashes grapefruit bitters**
- **2 dashes Rosemary Tincture (see recipe)**

1. Combine all of the ingredients in a mixing glass with ice and stir thoroughly.
2. Double-strain the cocktail into a Nick & Nora and garnish with a rosemary sprig.

Vanilla Syrup: Combine 1 cup Simple Syrup (see recipe on page 18) and 5.625 grams vanilla paste in a bowl and whisk thoroughly. Store refrigerated for up to 3 weeks.

Rosemary Tincture: Combine 2 cups Everclear and 1 bunch fresh rosemary in a glass container, cover, and let the infusion sit overnight. Strain.

BEACH DON'T KILL MY VIBE

POKA LOLA SOCIAL CLUB
1850 WAZEE STREET, DENVER

When Poka Lola mixologist Lexi Parker decided to make her own toasted coconut rum, she also wanted to play around with the kiwi-esque flavors of the dragon fruit. This punch (with twenty-five servings—you'll want to make it for a crowd!) is fruity and coconuty without being too sweet or overpowering the whole drink like a Piña Colada might. "We've had it on the menu three summers in a row because guests love it so much," Parker says.

GLASSWARE: **Footed pilsner glass**
GARNISH: **Mint leaves**

- **½ liter Toasted Coconut Rum (see recipe)**
- **2¾ cups Don Q Cristal**
- **½ liter kiwi puree**
- **½ liter dragon fruit puree**
- **¼ bottle John D. Taylor's Velvet Falernum**
- **1¾ cups Simple Syrup (see recipe on page 18)**
- **5 drops Saline Solution (see recipe on page 19)**
- **½ liter fresh lime juice**

1. Combine all of the ingredients in a large bowl or pitcher and stir.
2. Fill a footed pilsner glass with ice, then pour in the punch.
3. Garnish with a mint bouquet and serve with a straw.

Toasted Coconut Rum: In a large container, combine 1 (750 ml) bottle of Don Q Cristal and 20 oz. unsweetened coconut flakes, toasted, and let the mixture sit overnight in the refrigerator. Strain through a fine-mesh strainer and store for up to 3 months.

RED SKIES AT NIGHT

STRANAHAN'S WHISKEY DISTILLERY AND COCKTAIL BAR
200 S. KALAMATH STREET, DENVER

Red Skies at Night is one of Stranahan's head mixologist Devin Ershow's favorite cocktails. Inspired by a late-afternoon Colorado hike when the setting sun cast a brilliant red hue over the mountains, Ershow thought of his mom who always says, "Red skies at night, sailor's delight!" Missing his family that evening, he created a recipe for people to enjoy during the holidays as they spend time with their loved ones. The big and bold flavors reflect the sunsets along the Front Range. Red Skies at Night uses Stranahan's award-winning Mountain Angel 10 Year, the brand's rarest release, and the first and only American single malt aged ten years in new charred American white oak casks.

GLASSWARE: Coupe glass
GARNISH: Manicured orange peel, Luxardo cherries

- 2 oz. Stranahan's Mountain Angel 10 Year
- ¾ oz. amaro
- ½ oz. Luxardo Maraschino Originale
- ½ oz. Cinnamon-Maple Syrup (see recipe)
- 2 dashes Fee Brothers Orange Bitters
- 2 dashes Fee Brothers Black Walnut Bitters
- Orange peel, to express

1. Chill a coupe glass. Combine all of the ingredients, except for the orange peel, in a mixing glass with ice and stir.

2. Strain the cocktail into the chilled coupe.

3. Squeeze an orange peel over the drink to express the orange oil over the cocktail, then discard the peel. Garnish with a manicured orange swath and Luxardo cherries.

Cinnamon-Maple Syrup: In a saucepan over medium heat, combine 8 oz. water, 8 oz. maple syrup, and 1½ cinnamon sticks. Bring the mixture to a boil. Lower the heat and simmer with the lid on for 20 minutes. Allow the syrup to cool, then strain.

WHISKEY MANGO FOXTROT

STRANAHAN'S WHISKEY DISTILLERY AND COCKTAIL BAR
200 S. KALAMATH STREET, DENVER

Think of this as a summery whiskey-based Margarita. The mango is perfectly refreshing and sweet for the season, and the spiciness of the Hatch chile-infused agave syrup nods to a favorite Colorado ingredient. Head mixologist Devin Ershow teamed up with Stranahan's tour guide Kevin Hommes to create this cocktail. The small batch of single malt whiskey used here is hand-crafted at high altitude and aged for four years in fifty-three-gallon, new American oak barrels with a #3 char.

GLASSWARE: Rocks glass

- **Tajín, for the rim**
- **1½ oz. Stranahan's Blue Peak Single Malt**
- **1 oz. mango nectar**
- **½ oz. fresh lemon juice**
- **½ oz. Pepper Agave Syrup (see recipe)**
- **3 dashes Hella Cocktail Co. Smoked Chili Bitters**
- **Dash Angostura bitters**

1. Coat half the rim and part of the side of a rocks glass with lemon juice and roll it in Tajín.
2. Combine the remaining ingredients in a cocktail shaker with ice and shake.
3. Add ice to the rimmed glass and strain the cocktail over the ice.

Pepper Agave Syrup: In a saucepot over medium heat, combine 18 oz. agave nectar, 9 oz. water, 1 sliced jalapeño with seeds, 1 sliced serrano with seeds, and 1 sliced Hatch green chile with seeds, and bring the mixture to a boil. Lower the heat and simmer, covered, for 20 minutes. Let the syrup cool and strain out the solids. Refrigerate for up to 3 weeks.

CHARLOTTE RUBALD, THE CRUISE ROOM

Whether you're new to Denver or a Colorado native, chances are you've been to—or plan to go to—The Cruise Room, in the historic Oxford Hotel. That says a lot about a bar that opened on December 6, 1933. (If that date jogs a memory, it might be because it was the day after Prohibition was repealed.)

The Cruise Room's long and narrow art deco room is lit by glowy red lights that shine upward from the floor and leave the banquets that line the wall in glorious shadow. It is, in a word, a vibe. And no matter if you visited decades ago or last night (the bar is Denver's longest-running drinking establishment), The Cruise Room experience remains largely unchanged.

There's a lot of lore surrounding a bar with such long-standing history, and almost no one gets it right. Lead bartender Charlotte Rubald laughs as she recalls all the tales she hears while on shift. "Just last night someone asked if the wall panels were from the *Titanic*," she says. Clearly not, since those, uh, would be at the bottom of the ocean. In reality the decor was inspired by the bar aboard the *RMS Queen Mary*, a British ocean liner that sailed the Atlantic Ocean from 1936 to 1967.

Much of the charm of The Cruise Room is the sense that when you slide into a booth or onto a bar stool, you're stepping back in time. "There's a suspension of reality when you walk in here," Rubald says. "It's kinda like cocktail history, which is fun and nerdy and beautiful—and pretty impossible to verify."

FIRE ON THE LI RIVER

THE CRUISE ROOM
1600 17TH STREET, DENVER

One of The Cruise Room's bartenders named this cocktail after the Li River, which runs through China's Guangxi Province. The river travels through a stunningly beautiful landscape marked by mythical-looking karst mountains that seem to have sprung straight from the pages of a fairytale. For the spicy tincture, the staff labels each batch based on its heat. "It's a nice hack for Spicy Margaritas and other cocktails," lead bartender Charlotte Rubald says. This provides a consistent way to make something spicy without dirtying a tin with muddling chiles without knowing how spicy they're going to be.

GLASSWARE: Coupe glass
GARNISH: Cilantro leaf

- **Salt, for the rim**
- **Black sesame seeds, roasted, for the rim**
- **2 oz. vodka**
- **¾ oz. fresh lime juice**
- **¾ oz. Simple Syrup (see recipe on page 18)**
- **Bunch cilantro**
- **Bunch mint**
- **4 dashes Bird's-Eye Chile Tincture (see recipe)**

1. Wet the rim of a coupe glass then dip the rim in salt and toasted black sesame seeds.

2. Combine the remaining ingredients in a cocktail tin with ice and shake.
3. Double-strain the cocktail into the rimmed coupe, and garnish by floating a cilantro leaf on top.

Bird's-Eye Chile Tincture: In a container, pour 1 (1 liter) bottle of Everclear over 1 quart bird's eye chiles, roughly chopped, and let the infusion sit for at least a few hours. Strain and store the tincture in dasher bottles. Note each batch's spiciness varies because of the ever-changing nature of the chiles.

DIRTY DEEDS

SOMEBODY PEOPLE
1165 SOUTH BROADWAY, #104, DENVER

There is something divinely special about Somebody People, Sam and Tricia Maher's plant-based restaurant that opened on South Broadway in 2019. The vibe is beach-cool meets David Bowie (the name, "Somebody People," comes from a Bowie song). The menu is always bright, seasonal, and somehow familiar. "The Dirty Deeds sits at the cross-section of my love for Martinis and my disdain for Dirty Martinis," says Somebody People bartender Holden Haddock. "I wanted to create a cocktail that offers similar spirit-forward complexity to other classic Martinis, like a Tuxedo or a Vesper, but features the same savory qualities and dinner-pairing potential as a traditional gin Dirty Martini."

GLASSWARE: Coupe glass
GARNISH: 3 skewered Castelvetrano olives

- **1 oz. aquavit**
- **1 oz. dry vermouth**
- **1 oz. olive brine**
- **½ oz. vodka**
- **½ oz. gin**
- **2 dashes Fee Brothers Celery Bitters**

1. Combine all of the ingredients in a cocktail shaker tin with ice and shake until very cold.
2. Double-strain the cocktail into a coupe and garnish with 3 skewered Castelvetrano olives.

GINGER LYTE (NA)

SOMEBODY PEOPLE
1165 SOUTH BROADWAY, #104, DENVER

The Mahers— Sam and Tricia, co-owners—quit drinking during the pandemic but have slowly worked wine and low-ABV cocktails back into the mix. And so it's no surprise that the nonalcoholic cocktails are excellent. "They aren't just cocktails without the alcohol," says Tricia. "Just like our food, we create and craft drinks that are meant to stand on their own, not as an afterthought. When Nick Smedley, Somebody People's bar manager, set out to create a nonalcoholic mule, he leaned on fresh ginger syrup and a bright, citrusy nonalcoholic spirit to replicate that classic ginger beer kick. The result is a bright, refreshing Highball. Note: A juicer is helpful when making this cocktail.

GLASSWARE: Collins glass
GARNISH: Dehydrated lime wheel

- **1¾ oz. Dhōs Non-Alcoholic Gin**
- **¾ oz. fresh lime juice**
- **½ oz. Ginger Syrup (see recipe)**
- **Soda water, to top**

1. Combine all of the ingredients in a collins glass with ice.
2. Garnish with a dehydrated lime wheel.

Ginger Syrup: Use a juicer to juice fresh ginger, as needed, then strain the juice through a fine-mesh strainer to remove any solid particles. Combine the ginger juice and an equal amount of Simple Syrup (see recipe on page 18).

QUETZALCOATL

MIDDLEMAN
3401 EAST COLFAX AVENUE, DENVER

Tasked with creating a tiki menu immediately after launching a spring-summer menu, bar manager Celeste Rangel-Ruiz headed down to Middleman's basement to look at what she had in stock that would fill the tiki need in an unexpected way. Thus, the *Quetzalcoatl*, "Feathered Spirit" in the Aztec language Nahuatl, came to light. "I was really relieved that the cocktail turned out as good as it did," she says. "I originally served it on crushed ice, but I personally like it better served up in the sour glass."

GLASSWARE: Sour glass
GARNISH: Dehydrated Pineapple (see recipe)

- **1½ oz. Jones House Vodka**
- **¾ oz. Lemon-Clove-Guajillo Honey (see recipe)**
- **¾ oz. Pineapple-Infused Amaro Sfumato (see recipe)**
- **¼ oz. Casa D'Aristi Xtabentún Honey & Anise Liqueur**
- **3 dashes Fee Brothers Fee Foam**

1. Combine all of the ingredients in a cocktail tin with ice and shake.
2. Double-strain the cocktail into a sour glass.
3. Garnish with the Dehydrated Pineapple that was used to infuse the Amaro Sfumato.

Lemon-Clove-Guajillo Honey: In a saucepan over medium-low heat, combine equal parts honey and water. Add 10 cloves and 3 dry guajillo chiles and steep over low heat, until you achieve the flavor you want. Strain and let the syrup cool.

Pineapple-Infused Amaro Sfumato: In a large container, combine fresh pineapple slices, cut into half-moons, as needed, and 1 bottle Amaro Sfumato, and let the infusion sit for 24 hours. Strain, reserving pineapple for the Dehydrated Pineapple garnish.

Dehydrated Pineapple: Place the pineapple reserved from the Pineapple-Infused Amaro Sfumato recipe in a dehydrator at 135°F until the rings are no longer chewy, about 12 hours.

OH MY LÖRT

MIDDLEMAN
3401 EAST COLFAX AVENUE, DENVER

I love Malört, but I've always thought of it as an incomplete amaro," bar manager Celeste Rangel-Ruiz says, explaining she feels like the spirit comes across as one-note. For this cocktail, she wanted Malört to drink rounder, something she achieved by working in Golden Falernum and a totally bizarre simple syrup. Rangel-Ruiz ended up entering the drink into a cocktail competition in Kansas City. Because she was on the road, she threw together the simple syrup without measurements.

GLASSWARE: Coupe glass
GARNISH: Burnt Lemon Wheel (see recipe)

- **1½ oz. Jeppson's Malört**
- **1 oz. Old Style Beer Simple Syrup (see recipe)**
- **½ oz. The Bitter Truth Golden Falernum Liqueur**

1. Combine all of the ingredients in a cocktail shaker tin with ice and shake.
2. Double-strain the cocktail into a coupe.
3. Garnish with a Burnt Lemon Wheel.

Old Style Beer Simple Syrup: This one is up to bartender interpretation. "I did it at an Airbnb, and instead of water I used Old Style beer, and added chamomile. I think it was like 10 tea bags to a whole 12 pack of beer, and a container of sage, half of a deli of sugar, and I just watched it on low heat because I wanted the right consistency but I didn't want it to get bitter."

Burnt Lemon Wheel: Quickly grill spent lemon husks and wheels and dehydrate them in the dehydrator at 135°F for 6 to 8 hours. "Since people think Malört tastes like burnt tires," Rangel-Ruiz says, "for the competition, I made the lemon wheels look like wheels with edible silver paint."

STUART JENSEN AND ALEX JUMP, PEACH CREASE CLUB

When the eighteen-hundred-square-foot Peach Crease Club opens across from the Mission Ballroom in 2025, it will mark the union of two of the biggest forces in Colorado's cocktail scene—professionally, that is. The power couple that is Stuart Jensen and Alex Jump got hitched in 2024. This new bar celebrates their first official project together.

But first, a little about them.

Jensen, co-owner of Curio Bar in Denver Central Market and Roger's Liquid Oasis in Edgewater Public Market, began his hospitality career cooking on the line. When Jensen took a side job barbacking at the speakeasy Green Russell, the energy of the bar grabbed him and never let go. "Bartending is not about knowing every recipe or every spirit, it's about a well-timed joke or an open ear when you need a little company," he told *Eater* in 2014.

Jensen eventually became the opening bar manager for chef Alex Seidel's Mercantile Dining & Provision when it opened in Union Station in 2014. Because of his background, Jensen often approaches bartending from a culinary perspective—a skill that many fellow barkeeps value.

Meanwhile, Jump, who is a native of Chattanooga, Tennessee, came to Denver in 2017 with the specific goal of working for the soon-to-open outpost of Death & Co. She was already a seasoned bartender, having discovered the art of hospitality while interning at a wine shop in Florence, Italy, honing those skills in Chattanooga, and, once in Denver, notching time at RiNo Yacht Club and Mercantile Dining & Provision. Jump's skills and creativity landed her the job of bar manager on the opening team of—you guessed it—Death & Co. From there, the awards began to stack up: in 2019 she was a finalist for Bombay Sapphire's Most Imaginative Bartender, in 2020 she was nominated for Tales of the Cocktail Bartender of the Year, and in 2021, she nabbed a spot on *Forbes* 30 under 30 Food and Drink list.

Alex Jump winning Best U.S. Bar Mentor during the 18th Annual Spirited Awards during Tales of the Cocktail 2024 in New Orleans.

When the pandemic highlighted the industry's increasingly fragile mental health, Jump lent her talents to co-founding Focus on Health (that the organization shares the same acronym as the industry term Font of House, is very intentional). She left Death & Co in 2022 and has been freelancing as a bartender and prioritizing outreach to bartenders who are struggling with substance abuse ever since. In 2024, that effort was recognized on the international stage when Jump won Best U.S. Bar Mentor at Tales of the Cocktail in New Orleans. "It's nice to know that a bar mentor can be someone who isn't just mentoring through normal bar things, but other things as well," Jump says. "I would say it's the greatest recognition of my career."

As fans of the HBO series *The Outsider* might have guessed, The Peach Crease Club is named after the show's stripclub. Jump grew up close to where the show is set, and off the cuff, she and Jensen began calling their home bar by the same name. During the pandemic, the couple turned a backyard shed into one heck of a bar, stocked with everything you can imagine two high-profile bartenders sipping and mixing, plus a bevy of zero-proof options. "It became a joke that this was the coolest bar in Denver that no one could come to," Jump says.

Fast forward to 2024 when the RiNo project finally took shape and Jensen and Jump needed a name for their project. "We thought Peach Crease Club deserved its own place," Jump says. Jensen describes the forthcoming bar this way: "We have a good idea of what our strengths are, and the things we like doing. Peach Crease is intended to be approachable and not intimidating; it's a place that feels like us and our friends."

CHERRY

PEACH CREASE CLUB
4180 NORTH WYNKOOP STREET, SUITE 130, DENVER

This cocktail was crafted to showcase the vibrant flavor of fresh Colorado cherries at their peak ripeness, celebrating their natural sweetness and tang. By incorporating lacto-fermented cherry juice, Peach Crease Club demonstrates a sustainable method of preserving the fruit, allowing them to be enjoyed year-round. The addition of cherry vinegar and horseradish-infused *kirschwasser* enhances the fruit's complexity. Note: You need a SodaStream (or something similar) for this recipe.

GLASSWARE: Collins glass
GARNISH: Freeze-dried cherry powder

- **2¼ oz. Lacto-Fermented Cherry Juice (see recipe)**
- **2 oz. water**
- **1¾ oz. Highland Park 12 Year Scotch**
- **¼ oz. Horseradish-Infused Cherry Brandy (see recipe)**
- **¼ oz. cherry vinegar**
- **½ teaspoon Citric Acid Solution (see recipe)**

1. Dust a collins glass with freeze-dried cherry powder.
2. Combine all of the ingredients in a carbonation bottle and chill until very cold.
3. Carbonate the bottle. Then pour the cocktail over ice into the rimmed collins glass.

Lacto-Fermented Cherry Juice: Combine 2 cups pitted cherries, 3 tablespoons filtered and distilled water, 2 tablespoons honey, 2 tablespoons whey, and ¼ teaspoon salt in a mason jar, ensuring the cherries are fully submerged in brine. Let the infusion sit at room temperature for 48 hours, then move it to the refrigerator for 2 days. Blend the mixture, then strain it through a fine-mesh strainer.

Citric Acid Solution: In a glass container, combine 800 grams water and 200 grams citric acid powder and mix until the powder is dissolved.

Horseradish-Infused Cherry Brandy: Combine 1 (750 ml) bottle of Massenez Kirschwasser Cherry Eau de Vie and 90 grams freshly grated horseradish in a container and let the infusion sit at room temperature for 24 hours. Strain off the horseradish through a fine-mesh strainer.

MCLAIN HEDGES AND MARY ALLISON WRIGHT, YACHT CLUB

McLain Hedges and Mary Allison Wright's award-winning bar, Yacht Club, is actually a take-two effort. The first iteration was called RiNo Yacht Club and it opened inside The Source, which was Denver's first food hall, in 2014. The bar was freestanding in the middle of the great hall and, in truth, the location wasn't the couple's first choice. That said, their avant-garde bottle shop, The Proper Pour, was just a few steps away and the food hall provided a good entry into the scene. "We moved out here because we wanted to open a bar," says Wright. The couple, who used to be concert promoters, moved from Tennessee because they saw the direction Denver was going and they wanted to be part of the city's growth.

And so, they signed on at The Source and popped up a bar that served insanely inventive drinks inspired by drinking cultures around the globe. Cocktails with ingredients like marsala sangria syrup or yuzu and soju pushed the bounds of what Denver had seen and the bar quickly had legions of fans. But when the lease was up ("We always knew the space wasn't ours," says Wright), the couple closed up shop and spent years looking for a brick-and-mortar location they could make their home.

When Yacht Club opened in the Cole Neighborhood (and dropped "Rino" from the name) at the end of 2021, it felt like coming home for Wright and Hedges and their fans. Since the beginning, the name was tongue-in-cheek. "At The Source, we literally didn't have walls or doors and everyone was welcome at all times," Wright says. "Yacht Club was the anti-club club from its inception." The same is true of the hi-low dive bar she and Hedges have created. Here, in a space that feels oh-so them, surprising and brilliant cocktails sit alongside a menu of loaded hot dogs. "We don't take ourselves too seriously," says Hedges. "We're in the business of hospitality and fun."

Another fun twist (and a Yacht Club signature since the beginning) is the use of wine in the cocktails. The reason is twofold: "With wine, we're accessing a ton of different flavors, acids, textures, tannins, aromatics, softness. We're stretching flavors and playing with ABV levels," Hedges explains, saying it's time to break down the barrier between spirits and wine. This methodology is also a clever use of cross-utilization where wines that are open become an easy zero-waste ingredient.

It's this line of thinking and the come-as-you-are culture Hedges and Wright have cultivated that has landed the bar on the international stage. In 2023, Yacht Club was named on the 50 Best Bars in North America list and won the highly acclaimed Ketel One Sustainable Bar Award in 2023. A year later, it was crowned Best U.S. Cocktail Bar at Tales of the Cocktail Foundation Spirited Awards. This is high, and much deserved, praise for a bar that began in a food hall and has grown into its wonderful dive-bar self.

The People of

DED RECKONING

YACHT CLUB
3701 NORTH WILLIAMS STREET, DENVER

As Yacht Club co-owner McLain Hedges explains, the Ded Reckoning, which is redolent of agave, chocolate, and mole, is like a Vieux Carré took a trip to Oaxaca. "We're essentially doing an exact build on the classic but with inspiration coming from Mexico's rich history of cuisine and distillation," he says. The name is derived from the navigational term, "dead reckoning," referencing the process of calculating the current position of a moving object by using previously determined positions along with estimates of speed, heading, and time. The misspelling is a little cheeky and a bit more pirate than savvy sailor, but that's certainly on brand for Yacht Club.

GLASSWARE: Double rocks glass
GARNISH: Orange wheel

- 1 oz. mezcal
- 1 oz. blanco tequila
- 1 oz. Italian sweet vermouth
- ¼ oz. crème de cacao
- 2 dashes Bittermens Xocolatl Mole Bitters
- 2 dashes Regans' Orange Bitters No. 6

1. Combine all of the ingredients in a mixing glass with ice and stir for 10 to 15 seconds.
2. Strain the cocktail over a large cube into a double rocks glass.
3. Garnish with an orange wheel.

CHANGES IN ATTITUDE

YACHT CLUB
3701 NORTH WILLIAMS STREET, DENVER

Inspired by escapism, nostalgia, and a little bit of Jimmy Buffett, this tropical oasis of a Highball has all the building blocks of a beachside classic with some surprises. McLain Hedges likes to build this cocktail in batches of at least ten. "Being a milk punch, it's very shelf stable once finished and kept refrigerated," he says. The process is time-consuming but the results are delicious, and everyone will want seconds. For the scotch, use either a blended or a softer Speyside single malt.

GLASSWARE: Collins glass

- **1 oz. scotch**
- **1 oz. Sercial or Verdelho Madeira**
- **1 oz. pineapple juice**
- **¾ oz. fresh lemon juice**
- **¾ oz. Giffard Coconut Syrup**
- **¾ oz. water**
- **¼ oz. Giffard Banane du Brésil**
- **1 oz. buttermilk**

1. Combine all of the ingredients, except for the buttermilk, in a large container. In a separate large container, place the buttermilk.
2. Add the cocktail batch to the buttermilk and allow it to sit for 30 minutes. Rinse the dirty container and use it for straining.
3. Place a coffee filter in a strainer and place that over the rinsed container.
4. After sitting for about 30 minutes, the cocktail batch should have begun to separate or "break." Once this occurs, pour the batch into the coffee filter. Allow for the first bit to run off until the liquid is running through clear.

5. Take the liquid that has passed through and add it back to the batch, only reserving the clear liquid. Once all the liquid has passed through and is clear, discard the filter and its contents, seal up the liquid (milk punch) and keep it in the refrigerator to get cold.
6. Add the cold milk punch to a SodaStream (or something similar) and carbonate.
7. After carbonating, allow the punch to stabilize (5 to 10 minutes, or even overnight) before opening the top. The whey in the cocktail will create a heavier "head" or foam than a normal carbonated beverage, so it's best to let the initial agitation of the carbonation mellow out to avoid a mess. The goal is get the carbon dioxide to dissolve completely into the liquid, which produces integrated bubbles.
8. Pour gently over ice and enjoy.
9. Re-fizz the container every time you put it back in the refrigerator to keep maximum carbonation.

SILENT DISCO

MERCANTILE DINING & PROVISION
1701 WYNKOOP STREET, SUITE 155, DENVER

At Mercantile Dining & Provision in Denver's Union Station, the inspiration for Silent Disco came when general manager Mike Mitchell wanted to create a cocktail with multiple levels of flavor on all points of the palate, while utilizing saffron liqueur. The drink begins with the smokiness of mezcal and flows to a subtle acidity of the lime, balanced alongside the anise of Chartreuse. The saffron liqueur provides a complementary herbaceous note mid-palate before giving way to a subtle chile flavor.

GLASSWARE: Nick & Nora glass
GARNISH: Lime half-moon

- 1 oz. Del Maguey Vida Clásico
- ½ oz. Yellow Chartreuse
- ½ oz. Apologue Saffron Liqueur
- ½ oz. fresh lime juice
- ¼ oz. Ancho Reyes Original Ancho Chile Liqueur
- ¼ oz. agave nectar

1. Combine all of the ingredients in a cocktail shaker. Add ice and shake until chilled.
2. Strain the cocktail into a Nick & Nora and garnish with a lime half-moon.

KYOTO LEMONADE

MERCANTILE DINING & PROVISION
1701 WYNKOOP STREET, SUITE 155, DENVER

While in Japan, general manager Mike Mitchell became fascinated with the traditional Japanese Highball, where a clean and simple focus allows the ingredients to speak for themselves. After returning stateside, Mitchell worked on this cocktail for three years. "I wanted to elevate the drink and really focus on the aromatics and the welcoming of spring," he explains. "Yuzu is *the* citrus of Japan and when ordering a lemonade cocktail in Japan, yuzu is used more prominently than lemon." In this cocktail, Mitchell blends Japanese gin with sake, but it's the rosemary simple syrup that pulls it together. For the sake, you can use any well-priced sake so long as it is a Junmai Ginjo style.

GLASSWARE: Collins glass
GARNISH: Rosemary sprig

- **1½ oz. Roku Gin**
- **¾ oz. Wakatake Onikoroshi Junmai Ginjo Sake**
- **¾ oz. yuzu juice**
- **½ oz. Lillet Blanc**
- **½ oz. Rosemary Syrup** **(see recipe on page 249)**
- **Lemon peel, to express**

1. Combine all of the ingredients, except for the lemon peel, in a cocktail shaker. Add ice and shake until chilled.
2. Add ice to a collins glass, then strain the cocktail into the glass.
3. Squeeze the lemon peel over the top of the glass to express its oils and discard.
4. Garnish with a rosemary sprig.

THE WILDFLOWER

WILDFLOWER
3638 NAVAJO STREET, DENVER

Inspired by LoHi, the historically Italian and Latino neighborhood within which Wildflower is nestled, The Wildflower is an embodiment of both cultures, tucked neatly inside an Old Fashioned glass. A twist on the traditional Italian Negroni, this drink utilizes Mexican components, such as mezcal and Granada-Vallet (a Mexican twin of Campari), and incorporates a beloved Italian amaro, Montenegro. Spirit-forward, herbaceous, and smoky, this cocktail has been a consistent crowd pleaser since the restaurant opened in late 2020.

GLASSWARE: Old fashioned glass
GARNISH: Orange twist, edible pansy

- **1¼ oz. Del Maguey Vida Clásico**
- **1 oz. Granada-Vallet Bitter Pomegranate Liqueur**
- **1 oz. Carpano Antica Formula Vermouth**
- **½ oz. Amaro Montenegro**

1. Combine all of the ingredients in a mixing glass over ice and stir to chill.
2. Strain the cocktail and over a large ice cube into an old fashioned glass.
3. Garnish with an orange twist and, if desired, an edible pansy.

BERGAMOT TODDY

WILDFLOWER
3638 NAVAJO STREET, DENVER

When the snow begins to fly each winter, Wildflower rolls out this Hot Toddy with a floral twist. The star ingredient, the very tart and bitter bergamot orange, can be difficult to source in the U.S. The good news is that the juice can be purchased online. In a pinch, you can substitute lemon juice, but the cocktail's flavor will be slightly modified.

GLASSWARE: Glass mug
GARNISH: Nutmeg, lightly toasted marshmallow

- **3 oz. apple cider**
- **1½ oz. Old Overholt Straight Rye Whiskey**
- **¾ oz. St. George Spiced Pear Liqueur**
- **½ oz. bergamot juice, plus more for misting**
- **¼ oz. Honey Syrup (see recipe on page 18)**
- **3 dashes walnut bitters**

1. Heat the apple cider until hot.
2. Add the remaining ingredients to the cider and stir.
3. Pour the cocktail into a glass mug.
4. Mist the cocktail with bergamot juice and dress with a zest of nutmeg, then garnish with a lightly toasted marshmallow.

EL CHUFACABRA

WILDFLOWER
3638 NAVAJO STREET, DENVER

The Chufacabra was inspired by a Wildflower employee who proudly prepares her family's tiger milk recipe for the restaurant's family meal. It's so good the bar staff decided to add rum and turn it into a cocktail.

GLASSWARE: Rocks glass

GARNISH: Horchata Rice Cracker (see recipe)

- **2 oz. Horchata de Chufa (see recipe)**
- **1 oz. Ron Zacapa No. 23**
- **1 oz. Coconut Cartel Blanco Rum**
- **¾ oz. Don's 3-to-1 Mix (see recipe)**

1. Combine all of the ingredients in a cocktail shaker with ice and shake until cold.
2. Strain the cocktail into a rocks glass and garnish with an horchata rice cracker.

HORCHATA DE CHUFA: Combine 1 liter water, 250 grams chufa nuts (tiger nuts), 75 grams sugar, and 10 grams cinnamon sticks in a blender and blend until grainy, then let the mixture soak overnight. Blend until smooth and milky. Strain the horchata through multiple layers of cheesecloth. Use within 2 days or freeze.

DON'S 3-TO-1 MIX: In a container, combine 3 parts Vanilla Simple Syrup (see recipe) and 1 part St. Elizabeth Allspice Dram.

Vanilla Simple Syrup: Prepare Simple Syrup (see recipe on page 18), and then add 1 vanilla bean to the syrup. Steep overnight. Strain out the bean and store the syrup in the refrigerator.

Horchata Rice Cracker: Cook 1 cup basmati rice in 3 cups water with 1 cinnamon stick until al dente, then allow the rice to cool. Remove the cinnamon stick. Blend until very smooth and thick (the mixture will thicken the more it blends. Using a high-powered blender is key). Spread the mixture into small rounds on Silpats or parchment paper and dehydrate at 145°F for 2 hours, flipping halfway through. Fry the crackers at 375°F in sunflower or neutral oil. This will make the cracker puff up. Allow them to cool and then coat them in Cinnamon Sugar (see recipe).

Cinnamon Sugar: Combine 1 cup sugar and 4 sticks cinnamon in a high-speed blender and blend until powdery. Store in an airtight container.

THE FRONT RANGE

Paloma

Neon Rainbow

Midnight in Jalisco

Butterfly Me to the Moon

Melon Sour

Tiki Negroni

High Plains

Bent's Fort Hailstorm Julep

Lavender Greyhound

Mable Gram

Bee's Knees

Broadmoor Cocktail

Annette Martini

Pera Speziata

Misirlou

Poco di Fuoco

What exactly is the Front Range? Now that's a question. The geographically and geologically inclined among us will tell you it's the swath of mountains that run from southern Wyoming to central Colorado. Some will simply say it encompasses anything east of the Continental Divide. And still others will explain that "the Front Range" is a general term that refers to the urban corridor that makes up the most populated parts of the state (aka the greater Denver metropolitan area, Colorado Springs, and Fort Collins). Taken together, all three of these definitions are, in their own ways, correct.

PALOMA

ROGER'S LIQUID OASIS
5505 WEST 20TH AVENUE, EDGEWATER

There once was a downtown bar called Brass Tacks. It opened in 2019 to great fanfare. The minds—Stephen Julia, Katsumi Yuso Ruiz, Stuart Jensen, and Zach Spott—behind the operation were stacked, but then 2020 hit. After two and a half years of navigating the pandemic and trying to keep afloat, the bar closed in October 2021. But in its short lifetime, Brass Tacks and its Paloma developed a cult following. Lucky for the devoted, the Paloma, which was served on draft for crisp, perfect carbonation, is available at Roger's Liquid Oasis in Edgewater.

GLASSWARE: **Collins glass**
GARNISH: **Grapefruit slice**

- **1½ oz. blanco tequila**
- **½ oz. fresh lime juice**
- **¼ oz. Aperol**
- **¼ oz. grapefruit juice**
- **¼ oz. Simple Syrup (see recipe on page 18)**
- **2 dashes Saline Solution (see recipe on page 19)**
- **3 oz. Squirt grapefruit soda, to top**

1. Combine all of the ingredients, except for the soda, in a cocktail shaker.
2. Strain the cocktail into a collins glass with ice and top with Squirt.
3. Garnish with a grapefruit slice.

NEON RAINBOW

ROGER'S LIQUID OASIS
5505 WEST 20TH AVENUE, EDGEWATER

"We almost always have a beer cocktail on the menu," says Stuart Jensen. "It's a fun way to bring in unique flavors and highlight Denver's reputation as a beer city." In this drink, the cantaloupe-esque flavor of Aelred Melon Liqueur really highlights the lush, tropical fruit and bright citrus notes in the hops. Neon Rainbow is the very definition of a summer sipper.

GLASSWARE: Collins glass
GARNISH: Lemon twist

- 1½ oz. Wild Turkey 101 Bourbon
- ¾ oz. fresh lemon juice
- ¾ oz. Honey Syrup (see recipe on page 18)
- ½ oz. Aelred Melon Liqueur
- West coast IPA, to top

1. Combine all of the ingredients, except for the beer, in a cocktail tin with ice and shake.
2. Strain the cocktail into a collins glass with fresh ice, and top with west coast IPA.
3. Garnish with a lemon twist.

MIDNIGHT IN JALISCO

SUNSET LOUNGE
111 CHESTNUT STREET, FORT COLLINS

Midnight in Jalisco is this Fort Collins rooftop bar's ode to nature's artistry. The bold and elegant cocktail was crafted to echo the serene beauty of a Colorado sunset. The core of the cocktail is reposado tequila, aged to perfection and reminiscent of twilight's depth. The spirit pairs seamlessly with the bright bitterness of Campari, whose radiant hue mirrors the fleeting brilliance of the evening sky. The rosemary-infused agave nectar is a fragrant nod to the lush mountain landscape that frames Fort Collins.

GLASSWARE: Coupe glass
GARNISH: Rosemary sprig

- **Black lava salt, for the rim**
- **2 oz. Olmeca Altos Reposado Tequila**
- **¾ oz. Campari**
- **¾ oz. Rosemary-Infused Agave Syrup (see recipe)**
- **¾ oz. fresh lime juice**

1. Wet the rim of a coupe then dip the glass in black lava salt to give it a rim.
2. Combine the remaining ingredients in a cocktail shaker with ice and shake well.
3. Double-strain the cocktail into the rimmed coupe. Garnish with a sprig of fresh rosemary.

ROSEMARY-INFUSED AGAVE SYRUP: Combine 2 cups agave nectar and 1 cup water in a saucepan and bring the mixture to a low boil. Remove from heat and add 5 to 7 sprigs of rosemary. Allow the syrup to steep for 12 to 24 hours, then strain.

BUTTERFLY ME TO THE MOON

SUNSET LOUNGE
111 CHESTNUT STREET, FORT COLLINS

Just as Frank Sinatra's melody spins a dreamlike tune, Butterfly Me to the Moon will take you on an elegant and beautiful journey. This cocktail experience perfectly captures the essence of Sunset Lounge: refined, timeless, and unforgettable.

GLASSWARE: Coupe glass
GARNISH: Lavender

- **1¼ oz. Lavender-Infused Gin (see recipe)**
- **¾ oz. fresh lemon juice**
- **¾ oz. Simple Syrup (see recipe on page 18)**
- **1 egg white**
- **¾ oz. Butterfly Pea Powder–Infused Gin (see recipe)**

1. Combine all of the ingredients, except for the Butterfly Pea Powder–Infused Gin, in a cocktail tin.
2. Dry-shake (without ice) until a nice foam forms; add ice and shake again.
3. Double-strain the cocktail into a coupe.
4. Use a barspoon to slowly float Butterfly Pea Powder–Infused Gin to achieve a nice layer of purple.
5. Garnish with lavender.

Lavender-Infused Gin: Add 1 cup lavender flowers into 1 (700 ml) bottle of Malfy Gin Originale and let sit for 1 hour. Taste and allow the infusion to sit longer for your desired lavender flavor. Strain the infusion through a cheesecloth and rebottle.

Butterfly Pea Flower–Infused Gin: Combine 3 tablespoons butterfly pea flower powder and 1 (700 ml) bottle of Malfy Gin Originale and let the infusion sit for 12 to 24 hours, until a dark purple color is achieved. Strain the gin through a cheesecloth and rebottle.

MELON SOUR

MARIGOLD
405 MAIN STREET, UNIT B, LYONS

For Marigold's opening menu in 2022, James Beard Award–nominated chef Theo Adley created a stellar small plate with compressed Charentais melon, split hazelnuts, chèvre, shiso, and a pickled onion, citrus, and sherry condiment. When Adley, who champions Colorado ingredients at the spectacular Lyons restaurant, reimagined the dish again this year, bar and spirits director Amy Hobbs knew she wanted to make a cocktail that paired with the plate. "This cocktail underscores our cocktail program's focus: culinary cocktails that reflect the local and seasonal ingredients the kitchen is celebrating," she says.

GLASSWARE: Coupe glass

- **1½ oz. Mijenta Blanco Tequila**
- **1½ oz. Salted Melon Juice (see recipe)**
- **¾ oz. fresh lemon juice**
- **½ oz. Henriques & Henriques Boal 10 Years Old Madeira**

1. Chill a coupe glass. Combine all of the ingredients in a cocktail shaker with ice and shake thoroughly.
2. Double-strain the cocktail into the chilled coupe.

Salted Melon Juice: Peel and cube 1 melon (preferably Charentais, but cantaloupe or orange-flesh honeydew melon work as well) and place it in a large bowl. Sprinkle the melon with 1 tablespoon Maldon Sea Salt Flakes and ¼ cup sugar, stir, and let the mixture sit for 3 hours. Blend, then strain the juice through a cheesecloth. Store it in the refrigerator in an airtight container for up to 4 days.

TIKI NEGRONI

MARIGOLD
405 MAIN STREET, UNIT B, LYONS

When I spent time in Paris in my twenties, the tiki bars there influenced my cocktail style," says bar and spirits director Amy Hobbs. "Many of my recipes have a tiki fundamental as their backbone. Take, for example, the grated nutmeg garnishing this Negroni riff. That's a classic finishing element for the Painkiller cocktail." Ever inspired by chef Theo Adley's menu, Hobbs created this cocktail with the restaurant's baba au rum cake in mind, but the gin initially overwhelmed the drink. Marigold's sommelier, Eric Bronson, rightfully suggested a coconut oil wash which helped soften the spirit's botanicals.

GLASSWARE: Double rocks glass
GARNISH: Grated nutmeg

- **1 oz. Coconut Oil–Washed Gin (see recipe)**
- **1 oz. Bitter Fusetti Banana**
- **1 oz. Casa Mariol Vermut Negre**
- **2 dashes Fee Brothers Black Walnut Bitters**
- **2 dashes Sirene Galanga Bitters**

1. Combine all of the ingredients in a cocktail mixing glass, add ice, and stir.
2. Use a julep strainer and strain the cocktail into a double rocks glass with ice.
3. Garnish with freshly grated nutmeg.

Coconut Oil–Washed Gin: Combine 4 oz. coconut oil and 1 (750 ml) bottle of Bordiga Occitan Gin in a freezer-safe container and freeze overnight. Strain and rebottle.

HIGH PLAINS

BASTA
3601 ARAPAHOE AVENUE, BOULDER

Traditionally, Mai Tais call for orgeat, an almond syrup used for texture and sweetness, but Basta bartender Robert Clark was looking for alternatives due to sustainability issues with the nut. One of the restaurant's classic dishes is a Caesar salad featuring crunchy pistachio in lieu of croutons. In a stroke of genius, the Basta team was able to reclaim pistachio trim (the pieces usually discarded before service) to build a base syrup. This Mai Tai riff leans on bright, savory pistachio and herbaceous aquavit rounded out by beet and rhubarb. The latter two ingredients are easy to come by locally in the spring and summer.

GLASSWARE: Double rocks glass

GARNISH: 2 to 3 drops Sage Oil (see recipe)

- **1½ oz. Norden Aquavit**
- **¾ oz. fresh lime juice**
- **½ oz. Beet-Rhubarb Syrup (see recipe)**
- **½ oz. Pistachio Orgeat (see recipe)**

1. Combine all of the ingredients in a cocktail shaker with ice and shake.
2. Dirty-pour (don't strain) the cocktail into a double rocks glass.
3. Garnish with Sage Oil.

Beet-Rhubarb Syrup: Juice ½ beet and up to 1 pound rhubarb, then strain the juices through a fine-mesh strainer and then again through a coffee filter. Weigh sugar to match the weight of the juice, and then combine the sugar and juices in a blender. Blend until the sugar is dissolved and incorporated. Store refrigerated for up to 2 weeks.

Pistachio Orgeat: Pulse 100 grams shelled and toasted unsalted pistachios in a food processor until fine (do not powder). Combine the pistachios, 300 grams sugar, and 300 grams water in a saucepan and heat until the sugar is dissolved. Simmer on low for 5 minutes, or until the mixture becomes a syrup. Steep for 12 to 24 hours. Strain and refrigerate.

Sage Oil: Combine 2 to 3 oz. oil and 6 to 8 large sage leaves in a blender and blend on high until the oil is warm. Allow the oil to cool.

BENT'S FORT HAILSTORM JULEP

THE FORT RESTAURANT
19192 CO-8, MORRISON

In the 1830s, at Bent's Fort, a historic fur-trading fort in southeastern Colorado, the favorite hot-weather drink was the Hailstorm. Enjoyed by trappers, voyageurs, and Native Americans alike, it's the earliest known mixed drink in Colorado, and is said to have been first made with the hailstones from a storm. Originally made with Monongahela whiskey from Pennsylvania or wheat whiskey from Taos, the cocktail resembles the classic Mint Julep we all know and love with fresh mint and a touch of sweetness. The Fort Restaurant in Morrison, which is a full-scale adobe replica of Bent's Fort, has been serving the Hailstorm Julep since opening in 1963. You can substitute scotch or cognac for the bourbon, if you prefer.

GLASSWARE: Wide-mouth pint mason jar
GARNISH: Sprig of mint

- 3 oz. bourbon
- 2 teaspoons confectioner's sugar
- 2 sprigs fresh mint

1. Combine the bourbon, sugar, and mint in the mason jar then fill the jar with ice.
2. Secure the lid and shake vigorously to release the mint's flavor and allow the ice to slightly dilute the drink.
3. Remove the lid and garnish with a sprig of mint.

LAVENDER GREYHOUND

THE ARVADA TAVERN
5707 OLDE WADSWORTH BOULEVARD, ARVADA

As beverage director Jason Patz puts it, The Arvada Tavern has a long history in Olde Town Arvada, and the inspiration for this cocktail is mostly lost to time. The building that houses the bar has been many things throughout the years, but first and foremost, starting in 1933, it was a bar. In fact, it was the first location in Arvada to legally serve alcohol. In 2012, Mike Huggins and Lenka Juchelkova took over the building and breathed new life into its historical bones. This drink recalls that refresh, and it has been a staple on the menu since Huggins and Juchelkova took over.

GLASSWARE: **Large coupe glass**

- **Lavender Sugar (see recipe), for the rim**
- **2 oz. fresh ruby red grapefruit juice**
- **1½ oz. vodka**
- **¾ oz. lavender syrup**
- **2 dashes Strongwater Lavender Bitters**

1. Wet half the rim of a large coupe glass then dip it in Lavender Sugar.
2. Combine the remaining ingredients in a cocktail tin with ice and shake.
3. Strain the cocktail into the rimmed coupe.

Lavender Sugar: Using a mortar and pestle, grind 2 tablespoons dried lavender flowers into a powder. Add 1 cup sugar and mix to incorporate. Store in an airtight container for up to 6 months.

MABLE GRAM

THE ARVADA TAVERN
5707 OLDE WADSWORTH BOULEVARD, ARVADA

As a long-standing bartender at The Arvada Tavern in the 1940s and 1950s, Mable Gram has legendary status. Gram's favorite cocktail was the Manhattan; this riff was created to pay respect and homage to her legacy.

GLASSWARE: Coupe glass
GARNISH: Cherry, lemon peel

- **2 oz. Rittenhouse Straight Rye Whiskey**
- **¾ oz. Dubonnet Rouge Grand Aperitif de France**
- **¼ oz. Yellow Chartreuse**
- **2 dashes Bittercube Cherry Bark Vanilla Bitters**

1. Chill a coupe glass. Combine all of the ingredients in a mixing glass with ice and stir.
2. Strain the cocktail into the chilled coupe.
3. Garnish with a cherry and lemon peel.

THE BROADMOOR

It's well defined that the Volstead Act, which put Prohibition into place on January 17, 1920, outlawed the national production and sale of liquor. But there was a pretty extensive loophole that made it legal to consume alcoholic beverages that had been purchased *prior* to the ban. Spencer Penrose, businessman and founder of the illustrious Broadmoor hotel and resort in Colorado Springs, intended to make the most of that wrinkle. (The son of a wealthy Philadelphia family, Penrose made his fortune in mining and ore production across the West, but he had dreamed of opening a luxury resort near Pikes Peak, the area's gallant 14,115-foot mountain.)

Getting around this clause took some forethought, especially since, in Colorado, Prohibition went into place four years ahead of the national ban. Nonetheless, Penrose spared no effort to stockpile stores of spirits at his personal estate in Colorado Springs and at the Broadmoor. Under Penrose's proud watch, while the rest of the country muddled through more than a decade of restrictions, there was never a dry day at the resort. There's little doubt that Penrose's foresight helped notch the luxury hotel, which had only opened in 1918, onto the places-to-go list of the well-heeled.

To this day, Broadmoor guests can wander Bottle Alley, a corridor outside of La Taverne, one of the on-property restaurants, for a glassed-in view of Penrose's extensive spirits collection that included Scotch, wine from Bordeaux, and bottles of Champagne. The oldest bottles date back to 1801, and many remain unopened.

BEE'S KNEES

LA TAVERNE, GOLDEN BEE,
HOTEL BAR AT THE BROADMOOR
15 LAKE CIRCLE, COLORADO SPRINGS

During Prohibition, "bathtub gin," the amateur spirit that was indeed often made in a bathtub, didn't exactly make for easy drinking. The additions of tart lemon juice and sweet honey smoothed out the rough edges and created a cocktail that lives on, albeit greatly refined, to this day. At the Broadmoor, the Bee's Knees is served in a coupe with an iced-down sidecar for refills.

GLASSWARE: Coupe glass
GARNISH: Lemon twist

- **2 oz. gin**
- **1 oz. fresh lemon juice**
- **1 oz. Honey Syrup (see recipe on page 18)**

1. Combine all of the ingredients in a shaker tin with ice. Shake until cold.
2. Strain the cocktail into a coupe and garnish with a lemon twist.

BROADMOOR COCKTAIL

SUMMIT AT THE BROADMOOR
15 LAKE CIRCLE, COLORADO SPRINGS

In 2018, the Broadmoor's lead bartender, Dennis Schuler, created this cocktail for the resort's centennial celebration. The drink tips its hat to the Bee's Knees, but gets a modern Martini touch.

GLASSWARE: Martini glass
GARNISH: Lemon twist

- **1½ oz. Old Overholt Straight Rye Whiskey**
- **¾ oz. fresh lemon juice**
- **½ oz. Honey Syrup (see recipe on page 18)**
- **¼ oz. Bénédictine**
- **Dash Angostura bitters**

1. Chill a martini glass. Combine all of the ingredients in a shaker tin, add ice, and shake.
2. Strain the cocktail into a chilled martini glass and garnish with a lemon twist.

ANNETTE MARTINI

ANNETTE
2501 DALLAS STREET, SUITE 108, AURORA

Annette is named after James Beard Award–winning chef Caroline Glover's great aunt Netsie. "Most of my memories of Netsie involve her sneaking me olives from her gin Martinis," Glover says. "When we opened Annette, I knew we had to have a really beautiful and well-balanced Martini on the menu." Glover and her husband, Nelson Harvey, turned to McLain Hedges of Yacht Club to develop that perfect cocktail, and it has lived on the menu ever since Annette opened in 2017.

GLASSWARE: Coupe glass
GARNISH: Olive

- **1 oz. Leopold's Navy Strength Gin**
- **1 oz. Dolin Dry Vermouth**
- **½ oz. Salers Gentian Apéritif**
- **1 teaspoon pear brandy**
- **Lemon peel, to express**

1. Chill a coupe glass. Combine all of the ingredients, except for the lemon peel, in a mixing glass and stir over ice.
2. Strain the cocktail into the chilled coupe.
3. Garnish with an olive. Express a lemon peel (squeeze the peel to release the oils) over the cocktail, then discard the peel.

PERA SPEZIATA

PIZZERIA ALBERICO
1730 PEARL STREET, BOULDER

Locals still call Pizzeria Alberico "Pizzeria Locale" (the original name when Frasca Hospitality Group opened the Italian spot next to Frasca Food and Wine in 2011). But no matter what you call it, the pizza and Italian dishes within remain excellent. The cocktails are an equal draw, and when bartender Gisella Rainsford was messing around with Moscow Mule riffs, she landed on this perfect Italian fall drink.

GLASSWARE: Double rocks glass
GARNISH: Cinnamon, dehydrated lime wheel

- **1 oz. Evan Williams Bourbon**
- **1 oz. Pear Cinnamon Syrup (see recipe)**
- **¾ oz. fresh lime juice**
- **¾ oz. Campari**
- **Soda water, to top**

1. Combine all of the ingredients, except for the soda water, in a cocktail shaker with ice and shake thoroughly.
2. Double-strain the cocktail into a double rocks glass. Fill with ice and top with soda water.
3. Garnish with a pinch of cinnamon and a dehydrated lime wheel.

PEAR CINNAMON SYRUP: Prepare Simple Syrup (see recipe on page 18), rendering down 1 pear in a pot of hot simple syrup with a cinnamon stick. Cool, strain, and store the syrup in an airtight container for up to 2 weeks.

MISIRLOU

TRAVELING MERCIES
2501 DALLAS STREET, SUITE 311, AURORA

The idea for Misirlou came to Traveling Mercies bar manager Zachary King when he was studying the origin of cocktails all the way back to the British East India Company. "In the explosion of craft cocktails that we've experienced for the last ten to fifteen years, I think a lot of people have forgotten the history of cocktails and, in some senses, lost sight of the origins of our trade in the name of doing things differently," King says. "I wanted this cocktail to be pretty deeply rooted in history and to reflect what a punch might have been like back in the 1600s." This cocktail is clarified, which might seem like a heavy lift for the home bartender, but anyone can do it—clarifying a cocktail softens the flavors of the spirit. (The milk proteins bind to certain molecules associated with bitter and astringent tastes, and when the milk curds are filtered out of the cocktail those bound up molecules are filtered out too.) Tip: when the punch is being collected one drop at a time, you're on the right track for total clarification.

GLASSWARE: **Double rocks glass**

- **1 oz. Batavia-Arrack van Oosten**
- **1 oz. Leopold's Navy Strength American Gin**
- **½ oz. Angostura bitters**
- **¼ oz. Clément Mahina Coco Liqueur**
- **1 oz. blood orange juice**
- **¾ oz. fresh lemon juice**
- **½ oz. Afghan Tea Syrup (see recipe)**
- **1½ oz. milk**

1. Combine all of the ingredients, except for the milk, in a cocktail shaker.
2. Place the milk in a separate vessel and pour the cocktail over the milk. Let it rest for at least 30 minutes at room temperature.
3. Steadily pour the cocktail through two coffee filters fitted into a fine-mesh strainer over a separate vessel. The milk curds will create a dense wall against the coffee filter, creating a layer of filtration that (when done correctly) will retain all of the solids, resulting in a cocktail that is perfectly clear.
4. When you think the cocktail is running perfectly clear, quickly and carefully switch the vessel that you are collecting the filtered liquid in and return any liquid to the original batch to be filtered again.
5. Pour the cocktail into a double rocks glass with a big cube of clear ice.

Afghan Tea Syrup: In a small saucepan over medium heat, combine 4 oz. sugar and 2 oz. water. Lightly crush 3 to 4 green cardamom pods and add them to the saucepan. Add 1 teaspoon loose oolong tea and a pinch of salt. Bring the mixture to a gentle simmer, stirring to dissolve the sugar. Simmer for 10 to 12 minutes, then remove the syrup from heat and strain out the tea leaves and cardamom pods. Let the syrup cool before using.

POCO DI FUOCO

FRASCA FOOD AND WINE
1738 PEARL STREET, BOULDER

To say that Michelin-starred Frasca Food and Wine is an Italian restaurant is an understatement. The food and wine menus are inspired by the Friuli-Venezia Giulia region in northeast Italy and, even twenty years after opening, the restaurant remains one of the most coveted reservations in Colorado. So it might seem off-brand that the *Poco di Fuoco*—the name is a Spanish-Italian mashup meaning "a little bit of fire"—was inspired by the not-at-all-Italian Margarita. With Suerte Tequila (created by Boulder locals Laurence Spiewak and Lance Sokol) as the main spirit, the drink is refreshing, while also carrying warm winter spice, citrus, and habanero heat. This delicious surprise is a Frasca original, and it's off the menu, but always available if you ask.

GLASSWARE: Double rocks glass
GARNISH: Grapefruit peel, grated cinnamon

- **1½ oz. Suerte Blanco Tequila**
- **1 oz. grapefruit juice**
- **½ oz. agave nectar**
- **½ oz. Cinnamon-and-Thai Pepper–Infused Vermouth (see recipe)**
- **¼ oz. Licor 43**
- **2½ droppers Bittermens Hellfire Habanero Shrub Bitters**
- **Splash lemon juice**

1. Combine all of the ingredients in a cocktail tin with ice and shake.
2. Strain the cocktail into a double rocks glass with fresh ice.
3. Garnish with grapefruit peel and grated cinnamon

Cinnamon-and-Thai Pepper–Infused Vermouth: Coarsely grind 20 grams cinnamon sticks and 20 grams dried Thai long pepper in a mortar and pestle. Toast the mixture in a pan until aromatic, about 1 minute. In a large glass container, combine 1 (750 ml) of Poli Gran Bassano Bianco Vermouth with the toasted cinnamon and long pepper and steep for 4 hours at room temperature. Refrigerate overnight. Strain the infused vermouth through either a coffee filter or cheesecloth and store in the refrigerator for up to 1 month.

THE MOUNTAINS

The Maxwell

Li'l A-Frame

Pink Parry

A-Frame Club's Après-Ski Set

Bacon Bloody Mary

The Looking Glass

Valentina Verde

Peach Sweetwater

The Persian Prince (NA)

Dirty Mary

Saved by the Bell

Frida's Crystal Ball

Colorado Cobbler

Chili Chai Ball

Rogue Planet

We Be Yammin'

Jeff's Family Tree

Clifford Griffin

Baby Doe Tabor

The Brakeman

New Boot Goofin'

Shooting Star Spritz

Lamplighter

Punch and Toddy

Champagne or Death

HayRyed

Yellow Pages

Dead Flowers

Lando

The Flatliner

Rippers Repose

Fennel & Rosemary Rickey

Tipsy Carrot

Harvest Moon (NA)

Haiku Spritz

Metanoia

Celtic Kantharos

Tell anyone in Denver that you're headed to the mountains, and the assumption is that you're referring to the resort towns on the western side of the Continental Divide, most likely Winter Park, Breckenridge, Vail, Steamboat, or Aspen. But say the same thing in Grand Junction, the largest city in western Colorado, and it probably means you're headed to Telluride, Ouray, or Powderhorn ski resort. The truth is, Colorado has roughly two hundred mountain towns and, depending on who you ask, anywhere from eighteen to twenty-eight mountain ranges running through the state. (The state is also the highest in the nation, with every inch of it sitting three thousand feet and above in elevation.) In short, "the mountains" is used as shorthand for "a getaway." Unless you live there; then "the mountains" just means you're home.

THE MAXWELL

A-FRAME CLUB
1008 WINTER PARK DR., WINTER PARK

Mixologist and Colorado native Max Williams grew up in Winter Park, the same ski town where the A-Frame Club, a mid-century-modern retreat with thirty-one A-Frame cabins, is located. When creating cocktails, he strives to include flavors that are Colorado-esque. Poblano chile, while not native to Colorado, is a staple ingredient in dishes from all over Colorado and New Mexico. Spring44 is a gin local to the town of Loveland, an hour north of Denver. This sipper is the perfect refresher after a day spent outside.

GLASSWARE: Coupe glass
GARNISH: Dehydrated lemon wheel

- **1½ oz. Spring44 Gin**
- **½ oz. Chareau**
- **½ oz. Ancho Reyes Verde Chile Poblano Liqueur**
- **½ oz. fresh lemon juice**
- **½ oz. Simple Syrup** **(see recipe on page 18)**

1. Combine all of the ingredients in a cocktail shaker, add ice, and shake.
2. Double-strain the cocktail into a coupe and garnish with a dehydrated lemon wheel.

LI'L A-FRAME

A-FRAME CLUB
1008 WINTER PARK DR., WINTER PARK

As a proud Colorado native, bar manager Sarah Gerberding has tried to include as many Colorado-based wines and spirits in the A-Frame's repertoire as possible. She also has an eye for organic, biodynamic, and ecologically friendly companies, such as MEII Vodka, which is zero-waste, additive-free, and distilled in Hotchkiss on Colorado's Western Slope. This bright, spirit-forward Martini is a lovely sipper that uses a classic French aperitif wine and two Colorado-based spirits. This cocktail is a lovely light start to a mountain evening.

GLASSWARE: Coupe glass
GARNISH: Lemon twist

- **¾ oz. Lillet Blanc**
- **¾ oz. MEll Zero Waste Vodka**
- **¼ oz. Jones House Orange Liqueur**

1. Combine all of the ingredients in a cocktail shaker, add ice, and shake.
2. Double-strain the cocktail into a coupe and garnish with a lemon twist.

PINK PARRY

A-FRAME CLUB
1008 WINTER PARK DR., WINTER PARK

Alex Dumas made their home in Colorado six years ago and since then has made the most of every sport, friend, food, and beverage the state has had to offer. Dumas, who is A-Frame Club's resident flavor genius, dreamed up this cocktail while thinking about winter and wanting to pair the classic seasonal flavors of pomegranate and cinnamon with tequila. The name is a nod to Parry Peak at sunset, which you can see from Winter Park.

GLASSWARE: Rocks glass
GARNISH: Ground cinnamon, pomegranate seeds

- 2 oz. reposado tequila
- ¾ oz. fresh lime juice
- ¾ oz. egg white
- ¾ oz. Honey Cinnamon Simple Syrup (see recipe)
- ½ oz. 100% pomegranate juice
- ¼ oz. Luxardo Bitter Bianco

1. Combine all of the ingredients in a Boston shaker and top with ice. Shake vigorously for 20 seconds.
2. Strain the cocktail into a rocks glass, fill remainder of the glass with ice, and garnish with ground cinnamon and pomegranate seeds.

HONEY CINNAMON SIMPLE SYRUP: Make Honey Syrup (see recipe on page 18), adding 5 cinnamon sticks to steep. Strain before using.

A-FRAME CLUB'S APRÈS-SKI SET

A-FRAME CLUB
1008 WINTER PARK DR., WINTER PARK

None of these combos are new cocktails. In fact, they are all ubiquitous to 1970s cocktail culture. That fits Winter Park's retro-cool A-Frame Club just right. In the spirit of the disco era, bar manager Sarah Gerberding added these cocktail sets to the après-ski menu to help transport everyone back to the 1970s.

GLASSWARE: Coupe glass

START WITH THIS BASE:

- **1 oz. crème de cacao**
- **1 oz. heavy cream**

ADD ONE OF THESE:

- **1 oz. Galliano for the Golden Cadillac**
- **1 oz. Crème de Noyaux for the Pink Squirrel**
- **1 oz. Crème de Menthe for the Grasshopper**
- **1 oz. Brandy for the Brandy Alexander**

AND FOLLOW THESE DIRECTIONS:

1. Combine crème de cacao, heavy cream, plus your liquor of choice in a cocktail shaker, top with ice, and shake.
2. Double-strain the cocktail into a coupe.

BACON BLOODY MARY

ARAPAHOE BASIN'S 6TH ALLEY BAR & GRILL
28194 US-6, DILLON

If you're a skier or a snowboarder, there is no place more Colorado than Arapahoe Basin, a ski area tucked up against the Colorado Divide and known for its extreme terrain. And just like the resort itself, the Bacon Bloody Mary served at the mountain's two bars is legendary. When the cocktail came to be circa 2010, bartenders at the base restaurant, 6th Alley Bar & Grill, initially infused bacon into vodka in-house. Demand quickly outstripped supply so the bar team partnered with Mile High Spirits in Denver to use the distillery's bacon-infused vodka in the famous beverage. During the 2023/24 ski season, the ski resort sold more than 30,000 Bacon Bloody Marys!

GLASSWARE: Imperial pint glass (20 oz.)

GARNISH: Bacon, pickle spear, olive, peperoncino

- Chile-lime seasoning salt, for the rim
- 3 oz. A-Basin Bacon-Infused Vodka (see recipe)
- ½ oz. Worcestershire sauce
- 3 shakes black pepper
- 3 shakes celery salt
- 3 dashes Tabasco
- Bloody Mary mix, to top

1. Wet the rim of an Imperial pint glass then dip the glass in chile-lime seasoning salt to give it a rim. Then add ice to fill the glass.
2. Add the remaining ingredients, then top with Bloody Mary mix. Pour the cocktail into another glass to mix, then pour back into the original, rimmed glass.
3. Garnish with a piece of bacon, a pickle spear, an olive, and a peperoncino.

A-Basin Bacon-Infused Vodka: In a large glass jar, combine 1 (750 ml) bottle of vodka and 1 cup warm bacon grease and stir. Let the infusion stand at room temp in a cool place for 2 weeks to 1 month. After 2 weeks, put the jar in the refrigerator so the grease solidifies. Poke a hole in the grease and drain the vodka out and discard the grease.

SAM REINKE, SNITCHING LADY DISTILLERY

There is no story more Colorado than that of Sam Reinke, lead bartender and bar manager of Fairplay's Snitching Lady Distillery. Originally from Wisconsin, Reinke followed the path of many Midwesterners and moved to Chicago after college. It was there that he found a passion for the craft beer scene.

This love of suds—and Reinke's wish to better understand and get closer to the beer-making process—led him to Colorado. Except, Reinke didn't stop in Denver, a hotbed of craft brewing, as one might have expected. No, he skipped right over the big city and moved straight to Fairplay, a tiny, historic mining town that sits at nearly ten thousand feet. If you're asking how many breweries could possibly exist in a town with a population of 740, the answer is one.

So what really drew Reinke to Fairplay? "People always ask, 'Why of all the places did you move from the Midwest straight to Fairplay?'" he says. "I love the mountains and my grandmother bought a cabin in 1980 that she sold to my parents, so we would spend our summers out here." The cabin is so rustic—there's no plumbing, heat, or electricity—that it's not livable year-round, but its many fond memories tied Reinke to the place. Plus, Fairplay is somewhat central to robust beer scenes: Breckenridge sits thirty minutes away, Buena Vista forty, and both Denver and Colorado Springs are less than two-hour drives.

The same year Reinke landed in Fairplay, Snitching Lady Distillery opened on Front Street, Fairplay's main drag. That was in 2018, and though Reinke had minimal experience, he landed a job behind the bar. "I feel like I've been able to grow with the distillery," he says. Snitching Lady also provided the platform for Reinke to really get to know the town. "Our local community is ranchers and the working class," he says. "It's an interesting dynamic because Fairplay is also a tourist town and without the tourist seasons, we couldn't do what we do."

So just what does Snitching Lady do? The distillery turns out rye, bourbon, and brandy, all drawing on the know-how of Thomas Williams, whose great-grandfather first started making moonshine in North Carolina. The spirits, which are crafted from Colorado fruit and grain (including blue corn from southwestern Colorado) are all double copper pot distilled right there on Front Street. As Reinke sees it, his job is easy because he's just adding to an already great product. "We love working with the agricultural community and the native population as well," he says. "For our brandies, we're a couple hundred miles from the Western Slope, which is the state's orchard region. We get to show off Colorado's diverse landscape."

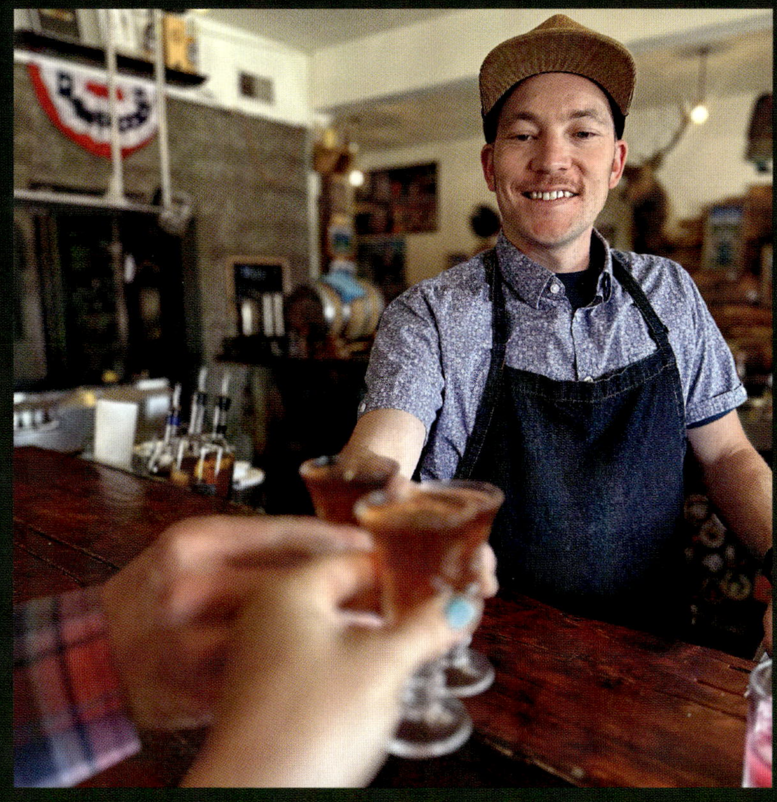

THE LOOKING GLASS

SNITCHING LADY DISTILLERY
500 FRONT STREET, FAIRPLAY

The tiny town of Fairplay (population 738) might be most famous for inspiring Trey Parker and Matt Stone's animated show *South Park*, but it was once a thriving gold mining town. Walk down Front Street, Fairplay's main street, and that history is proudly on display. Make your way to Snitching Lady Distillery, so named because owner Thomas Williams decided to make his backyard hobby legal so he didn't get snitched on. As bar manager Sam Reinke says, "So many of the cocktails we craft in our tasting room are whiskey based, but we also make delicious brandy that creates its own unique flavor profile when used in a cocktail." The Looking Glass is one such cocktail and it was inspired by the song "Brandy, You're a Fine Girl" by The Looking Glass.

GLASSWARE: **Coupe glass**
GARNISH: **Dehydrated pear slice**

- **1 oz. Snitching Lady Appalachian Temptation Grape Brandy**
- **¾ oz. Pear Simple Syrup (see recipe)**
- **½ oz. allspice dram**
- **½ oz. fresh lime juice**
- **¼ oz. dry vermouth**

1. Chill a coupe glass. Combine all of the ingredients in a cocktail shaker with ice and shake vigorously.
2. Strain the cocktail into the chilled coupe and garnish with a slice of dehydrated pear.

PEAR SIMPLE SYRUP: Make Simple Syrup (see recipe on page 18), adding 2 cups diced pears to the saucepan with the water and sugar. Simmer for 15 minutes, or until the pears soften enough to smash with a spoon. Stir occasionally. Strain and allow the syrup to cool.

VALENTINA VERDE

SNITCHING LADY DISTILLERY
500 FRONT STREET, FAIRPLAY

"The idea for this cocktail came to me late at night after closing the bar and after consuming several whiskeys," bar manager Sam Reinke says. "The thought was simply, 'Would avocado work in a cocktail?'" He immediately got to work, dreaming up a few different avocado-based creations. The fruit's creamy texture pairs perfectly with the buttery flavors of the distillery's blue corn whiskey. Add to that pistachio bitters (made by now-defunct Après Bitters in Breckenridge), and Reinke realized nearly every ingredient of the cocktail was green. The bar now serves the Valentina Verde every St. Patrick's Day and, even when it's not on the menu, it's one of the most-requested cocktails.

GLASSWARE: Tall decorative glass
GARNISH: Cilantro, jalapeño

- **1 large spoonful ripe avocado**
- **2 to 3 slices fresh jalapeño**
- **1½ oz. Snitching Lady Blue Corn Whiskey**
- **1 oz. Simple Syrup (see recipe on page 18)**
- **½ oz. fresh lime juice**
- **Fresh cilantro leaves, to taste, torn into small pieces**
- **Dash pistachio bitters**

2. Add the remaining ingredients and ice and shake vigorously.
3. Double-strain the cocktail into a tall decorative glass with crushed ice cubes.
4. Garnish with cilantro and jalapeño.

PEACH SWEETWATER

SNITCHING LADY DISTILLERY
500 FRONT STREET, FAIRPLAY

Every July, Fairplay celebrates its annual Burro Days, a festival that honors the burro's place in the town's mining history. The fest coincides with the ripening of Colorado's prized Palisade peaches, and bar manager Sam Reinke crafted a cocktail that celebrates both occasions. He combines Snitching Lady's "Burro-bon" bourbon with peaches, fresh basil, and a touch of balsamic to create the ultimate Colorado summer cocktail. And true to form, the distillery sells more of this cocktail than any other during Burro Days weekend in late July.

GLASSWARE: Rocks glass
GARNISH: Fresh basil leaves

- 1½ oz. Snitching Lady "Burro-bon" Bourbon Whiskey
- 1 oz. pureed fresh Palisade peaches
- ¾ oz. Simple Syrup (see recipe on page 18)
- ½ oz. fresh lemon juice
- ½ teaspoon balsamic vinegar
- 2 fresh basil leaves, torn into small pieces

1. Combine all of the ingredients in a cocktail shaker with ice and shake vigorously.
2. Strain the cocktail into a rocks glass over a large ice cube, and garnish with fresh basil leaves.

JEREMY CAMPBELL, ROOT & FLOWER

When Samantha Biszantz and Jeremy Campbell opened Root & Flower in the Vail Village in 2015, it was partly a selfish endeavor. "When Sam and I were working together at [the now closed] Restaurant Kelly Liken, people would say, 'This was such a great experience, now where should I go grab a drink?'" Campbell recalls. "There wasn't any place to recommend. That was something Vail was missing."

And so, the two put their heads together and created Root & Flower, a twelve-seat, high-end wine bar that *they* wanted to frequent for après-ski or a nightcap. "Root & Flower wasn't supposed to be just for Vail," Campbell says. "It was meant to be a place that you could throw into a city like Chicago or San Francisco and it would fit. We try to maintain that level of quality by doing a lot of R&D and traveling to compare and take notes."

Biszantz and Campbell might have framed Root & Flower as a high-level wine bar, but it immediately found a wider audience. "The funny thing is, we originally opened to be a wine bar but we're actually better known as a cocktail bar," Campbell says. "We're really both." Those twelve bar seats filled up every evening and it wasn't unusual, even in a snowstorm, to see a line of people waiting to get in. In 2019, Biszantz and Campbell moved to a location on Bridge Street that was three times the size.

THE PERSIAN PRINCE (NA)

ROOT & FLOWER
288 BRIDGE STREET, VAIL

This nonalcoholic cocktail was inspired by a typical summer sharab drink—or a tart vinegary shrub—dating back to eleventh-century Persia.

GLASSWARE: Collins glass
GARNISH: Cucumber, fresh mint

- **1-inch piece cucumber**
- **1½ oz. Honey Shrub (see recipe)**
- **½ oz. fresh lime juice**
- **5 mint leaves**
- **4 oz. soda water, to top**

1. Place the cucumber in a cocktail shaker and muddle it.
2. Add the remaining ingredients, except for the soda water, then add ice and shake thoroughly.
3. Double-strain the cocktail into a collins glass with fresh ice and top with soda water.
4. Garnish with a fresh slice of cucumber and mint.

HONEY SHRUB: In a saucepan over high heat, bring 1 cup honey and ½ cup water to a boil. Add ¼ cup white wine vinegar, bring the mixture to a boil again, then quickly remove it from heat. Add 2 bags of Steven Smith "Fez" Green Mint Tea, steep for 10 minutes, then remove and discard the tea bags. Store the shrub in the refrigerator for up to 2 months.

DIRTY MARY

ROOT & FLOWER
288 BRIDGE STREET, VAIL

This tomato-forward Dirty Martini borrows from the classic Italian cooking technique of *acqua pazza*. Translating to "crazy water," the term refers to a light broth. As with all things tomato, don't bother with this cocktail if the fruit is out of season.

GLASSWARE: Nick & Nora glass
GARNISH: Cherry tomato, basil leaf

- **2½ oz. Olive Oil–Washed Vodka/Vermouth (see recipe)**
- **¾ oz. Tomato Water (see recipe)**
- **3 dashes celery bitters**

1. Combine all of the ingredients in a mixing glass with ice and stir thoroughly.
2. Strain the cocktail into a Nick & Nora, then garnish with a cherry tomato and a basil leaf skewered on a pick.

OLIVE OIL–WASHED VODKA/VERMOUTH: Combine 1 (750 ml) bottle of Jones House Vodka, 100 ml Dolin Dry Vermouth, and 100 ml olive oil in a container and mix well. Cover and let the mixture sit overnight at room temperature, then put it in the freezer. Strain through a cheesecloth-lined strainer and discard any solids. Store refrigerated for up to 1 month.

TOMATO WATER: Dice ripe tomatoes, as needed, and weigh them. Take that weight and add 1.5% of that weight in salt to the tomatoes. Add fresh basil, finely chopped, and freshly ground pepper, to taste. Place all of the ingredients in a cheesecloth-lined strainer and let drip. Refrigerate overnight. Collect clear liquid, and strain any liquid with color through a coffee filter. Store it in the refrigerator for up to 3 days.

SAVED BY THE BELL

ROOT & FLOWER
288 BRIDGE STREET, VAIL

Created by one of Root & Flower's founding bartenders, Joe Newton, Saved by the Bell, which highlights the beauty of red pepper, has been a mainstay since 2019.

GLASSWARE: Double rocks glass

- **Tajín, for the rim**
- **1 oz. mezcal**
- **1 oz. reposado tequila**
- **1 oz. Red Pepper Shrub (see recipe)**
- **½ oz. Ancho Reyes Original Ancho Chile Liqueur**
- **½ oz. fresh lemon juice**
- **¼ oz. Chile de Árbol Simple Syrup (see recipe)**
- **¼ oz. Fernet-Branca**

1. Wet the rim of a double rocks glass, then dip the glass in Tajín to give it a rim.
2. Combine the remaining ingredients in a cocktail shaker with ice and shake thoroughly.
3. Strain the cocktail into the rimmed glass and top with fresh ice.

RED PEPPER SHRUB: Remove the stems and seeds from 2 red bell peppers. Weigh the cleaned peppers, then measure their weight and add 25% of that weight in sugar, and 25% of that weight in red wine vinegar. Combine all of the ingredients in a blender and blend until liquified. Strain and store refrigerated for up to 1 month.

Chile de Árbol Simple Syrup: Combine 1 cup white sugar, 1 cup water, and 4 dried chiles de árbol in a medium saucepan over medium heat. While stirring, bring the mixture to a boil. Immediately remove the syrup from heat and allow it to cool. Strain and store in the refrigerator for up to 1 month.

FRIDA'S CRYSTAL BALL

ROOT & FLOWER
288 BRIDGE STREET, VAIL

This show-stopping cocktail was created by Root & Flower alum JD Morris. As co-owner Jeremy Campbell says, "We fell in love with the drink's simplicity on paper and its complexity on the palate." Serving this cocktail over a clear sphere of ice completes the experience.

GLASSWARE: Rocks glass
GARNISH: Edible glitter

- **1 oz. mezcal**
- **1 oz. CapRock Pear Eau De Vie**
- **½ oz. Salers Gentiane Apéritif**
- **½ oz. Atxa Sweet White Vermouth**

1. Combine all of the ingredients in a mixing glass with ice and stir thoroughly.
2. Strain the cocktail into a rocks glass with a clear sphere of ice and garnish with a dash of edible glitter.

DEVIN ERSHOW, STRANAHAN'S WHISKEY LODGE

Devin Ershow, the head mixologist at Stranahan's Whiskey Lodge, personally favors classic cocktails like the Sazerac, but all of his whiskey-forward creations, served in Aspen and in Denver, are dynamic sippers. Get Ershow talking—he's also the CEO of American Mash & Grain, an independent whiskey journalism site—and you'll leave the bar steeped in newfound whiskey knowledge.

When Stranahan's Whiskey Lodge opened on Aspen's Mill Street pedestrian mall in March 2024, it was a homecoming for the Colorado whiskey brand. As the story goes, in 1998, volunteer firefighter Jess Graber got the call that a barn in Woody Creek (an unincorporated town eight miles outside of Aspen) was on fire. The barn, which ultimately burnt to the ground, was owned by George Stranahan, a longtime local who founded the legendary Woody Creek Tavern and owned Flying Dog Brewery.

That haphazard introduction led to a friendship and a mutual love of whiskey. Over time, the two hatched the idea to partner, create, and launch Stranahan's Colorado Whiskey, the state's first American single malt whiskey. In 2004, they opened a distillery in Denver, which was Colorado's first legal distillery since Prohibition. Stranahan's took off and two decades later, the whiskey is championed as top in its category and is the nation's most awarded American single malt.

And so, to mark its twenty-year anniversary, the brand came home. Stranahan's Whiskey Lodge, a cozy, warm hued bar, is an ode to all things Stranahan's with flights, craft cocktails, and bottles for purchase (some limited only to the Aspen location). Chef Nick Ragazzo's menu is designed to highlight the spirits (the freshly made pasta and pretzel hot pocket are highlights). There's even a framed black-and-white photo of namesake George Stranahan, who passed away in 2021, hanging on the wall.

COLORADO COBBLER

STRANAHAN'S WHISKEY LODGE
307 SOUTH MILL STREET, ASPEN

While the Sherry Cobbler is a refreshing summer cocktail served over crushed ice, Stranahan's Colorado Cobbler is a spirit-forward refresh of the classic. When head mixologist Devin Ershow created the cocktail, he intentionally made Stranahan's Sherry Cask the star. The small-batch American Single Malt whiskey is crafted from seven-year-old barrels and finished in oloroso sherry barrels.

GLASSWARE: **Coupe glass**
GARNISH: **Lemon curl**

- **1½ oz. Stranahan's Sherry Cask**
- **1 oz. sweet vermouth**
- **½ oz. orange curaçao**
- **2 dashes Fee Brothers Peach Bitters**

1. Chill a coupe glass. Combine all of the ingredients in a mixing glass with ice and stir.
2. Strain the cocktail into the chilled coupe.
3. Using a channel knife (a knife with a V-shape blade designed to cut citrus curls), cut a lemon curl over the glass to express the lemon oil over the drink. Twist the curl into a tight spiral and hang it on the rim of the glass.

CHILI CHAI BALL

STRANAHAN'S WHISKEY LODGE
307 SOUTH MILL STREET, ASPEN

"This recipe was originally designed for an Asian food pairing, and as a Highball, there was a great opportunity for a pun," head mixologist Devin Ershow says. The chai tea syrup includes beautiful warm spices, and because Colorado has a deep history with hot peppers, a smoky chile aspect is included in the bitters.

GLASSWARE: **Collins glass**
GARNISH: **Dehydrated lemon wheel**

- **1½ oz. Stranahan's Blue Peak Single Malt**
- **1 oz. Chai Syrup (see recipe)**
- **½ oz. fresh lemon juice**
- **4 dashes Hella Cocktail Co. Smoked Chili Bitters**
- **Ginger beer, to top**

1. Chill a collins glass. Combine all of the ingredients, except for the ginger beer, in a cocktail shaker with ice and shake briefly.
2. Strain the cocktail into the chilled collins glass.
3. Top with ginger beer and garnish with a dehydrated lemon wheel.

CHAI SYRUP: Add 8 oz. water to a pot and bring it to a boil. Turn off the heat and add 1 bag chai tea. Cover and let the tea steep for 30 minutes. Remove the tea bag and add 8 oz. sugar. Stir to combine over medium heat until the sugar is dissolved.

BILLIE KEITHLEY, BRECKENRIDGE DISTILLERY

Breckenridge Distillery's "liquid chef" Billie Keithley's bartending career began by accident. She was managing the front of the house at Salt Creek Steakhouse in Breckenridge when the scheduled bartender didn't show up because of a snowstorm. Keithley jumped in and, well, the rest is history. "I thought, 'Oh this is really cool, I want to take a shift myself.' I was just enthralled by the smells, the colors, of process of putting things together," she says. Granted, this was about twenty years ago, and Keithley was mostly serving pitchers of beer, Vodka & Red Bulls, and shots. Even so, she wanted to keep learning.

At about that time, a close friend who worked for a distributor invited Keithley to a cocktail seminar with Francesco Franconi, one of the world's most prominent mixologists. Keithley went to help her friend pad the room but didn't expect to learn much of anything. "I walked out of there with ten pages of notes," she says. "I realized I didn't know anything about this craft, but I knew that this is what I wanted to do."

Keithley began fiddling at home and experimenting with homemade syrups and shrubs—all of which she would bring to work. Her timing was impeccable. On a chance shift at Cecilia's Cocktail Bar & Nightclub in Breckenridge, she struck up a conversation with a couple customers on the other side of the bar. The guests, it turns out, were Bryan Nolt and Jordan Via, the CEO and master distiller, respectively, of the then-new Breckenridge Distillery. "We started talking about cocktails and spirits, and I made them some drinks," Keithley recalls. "They invited me to the distillery the next day. That was fifteen years ago."

The three, plus a couple other employees, joined forces and, in the grassroots way startups gain traction, they drove all over the state spreading the word about the distillery's bourbon, vodka, and bitters. At tastings and events, Keithley began showing up with cocktail makings. "I didn't want to just pour spirits," she says. "I made cocktails everywhere I showed up."

And when, in 2016, the "Breck Distillery" as it's called locally expanded to a second location and added a restaurant on the outskirts of town, Keithley suddenly had a platform. "They said, run with it. This is yours, we trust you," she says. And run with it she did: Breck Distillery has become known far and wide for its beverage program.

Keithley has found her calling, and even as she marks nearly two decades bartending, time hasn't dulled her creativity. "I don't stop learning," she says from her home lab in Steamboat Springs. "I have books everywhere. I'm constantly listening to podcasts. If I can think it, I can make it work. I'll draw out what a cocktail should look like and I'll send it to my team." Sometimes things get, as she says, "sciency." But that only underscores that sometimes things come full circle. "I still have my first science book," Keithley laughs. "It has my name on the inside front cover and it says. "If lost, please return. This is my favorite book."

ROGUE PLANET

BRECK DISTILLERY
1925 AIRPORT ROAD, BRECKENRIDGE

Billie Keithley is obsessed with *Star Wars,* so much that every menu she produces for Breckenridge Distillery includes at least once reference to the cinematic epic. The Rogue Planet features two of Keithley's favorite ingredients—fig and allspice—plus a brown butter wash for mouthfeel.

GLASSWARE: Double rocks glass
GARNISH: Bull's blood microgreens

- **2 oz. Brown Butter–Washed Bourbon (see recipe)**
- **2 oz. tart cherry juice**
- **1 oz. Allspice Syrup (see recipe)**
- **1 oz. fresh lemon juice**
- **¾ barspoon (¾ teaspoon) mission fig vinegar**

1. Combine all of the ingredients in a cocktail tin with ice and shake.
2. Strain the cocktail over ice into a double rocks glass and garnish with bull's blood microgreens.

BROWN BUTTER–WASHED BOURBON: In a saucepan over medium heat, melt 1 stick unsalted butter until it has a nutty aroma. Combine the melted butter with 1 (750 ml) bottle of Breckenridge Bourbon Whiskey in a glass pitcher and freeze the mixture overnight. Skim off the butter and strain. Store the whiskey in the refrigerator for up to 2 weeks.

Allspice Syrup: In a saucepan over medium heat, combine 1 cup water, 1 cup brown sugar, and 2 oz. allspice. Muddle the allspice and stir until the sugar is dissolved. Let the syrup cool, then strain, bottle, and refrigerate it for up to 1 month.

WE BE YAMMIN'

BRECK DISTILLERY
1925 AIRPORT ROAD, BRECKENRIDGE

Billie Keithley finds inspiration everywhere, but especially when walking through a grocery store's produce department and seeing what's available. On one such trip, she came across ube, a purple yam native to the Philippines, and knew she had to do something with it. "Ube has that tropical, tiki-esque flavor," she says. "The nuttiness is fun and inviting with our 105 High Proof, date, cardamom, and allspice."

GLASSWARE: Double rocks glass
GARNISH: Purple pansy

- **2 oz. Breckenridge High Proof 105**
- **1 oz. Date-Allspice-Cardamom Syrup (see recipe)**
- **1 oz. fresh lemon juice**
- **Ube Foam (see recipe), to top**

1. Combine all of the ingredients, except for the foam, in a cocktail shaker with ice and shake.
2. Strain the cocktail over ice into a double rocks glass and top with the ube foam.
3. Garnish with a purple pansy.

Date-Allspice-Cardamom Syrup: In a saucepan over medium heat, combine 1 cup water, ¾ cup date syrup, and ¼ cup brown sugar and stir until the sugar is dissolved. Add 1 oz. allspice berries, muddled or crushed, and ½ oz. cardamom seeds (removed from husk), muddled or crushed, and stir. Let the syrup rest for 2 hours. Strain, bottle, and refrigerate the syrup for up to 1 month.

Ube Foam: In a cream whipper canister, combine 10 oz. Ube Simple Syrup (see recipe) and 4 oz. egg whites. Charge the canister, shake, and refrigerate until ready to use.

Ube Simple Syrup: Make Simple Syrup (see recipe on page 18) with 1 cup water and 1 cup sugar, adding ½ oz. ube extract once the sugar is dissolved.

JEFF'S FAMILY TREE

AURUM FOOD & WINE
209 SOUTH BRIDGE STREET, BRECKENRIDGE

Even if the goal is to eat dinner at this innovative restaurant in Breckenridge, the most coveted place to sit is in the bar area. Here, the energetic bartenders never stop shaking, stirring, and serving drinks like the Jeff's Family Tree. The "Jeff" in this cocktail's name refers to Jeff Otterson, one of Aurum's long-time employees who worked his way up the ranks. Although Otterson has since moved on to become a level three sommelier in Napa Valley, he leaves his legacy behind in this cocktail. It's one Phil Armstrong, head of Destination Hospitality, the restaurant group that owns Aurum, always has the makings for in his home bar. "I batch it for every gathering," Armstrong says. "It's a huge fan favorite."

GLASSWARE: Double rocks glass
GARNISH: Orange twist

- 1 oz. Rittenhouse Straight Rye Whisky
- ¾ oz. Del Maguey Vida Clásico
- ½ oz. B&B By Bénédictine
- 2 dashes Peychaud's bitters

1. Combine all of the ingredients in a mixing glass with ice and stir.
2. Strain the cocktail over a big ice cube into a double rocks glass.
3. Garnish with an orange twist.

STEVE FENBERG, BREAD BAR

If the first tenet of business success is location, location, location, then Bread Bar should have shuttered long ago. Instead, the bar, which opened in the teeny mountain town of Silver Plume in July 2013, has flourished. The former mining camp is home to roughly two hundred residents, and is as about unlikely a place to host a hipster bar owned by four city-living friends as you can imagine. "Silver Plume isn't just a small town," says co-owner Steve Fenberg. "It's a small town that likes to be left alone. There's no police force, they've never paved the roads, and they have to beg people to run for mayor." And yet, over the years, the town has embraced Bread Bar as its living room.

It works, in part, because of the building itself, which is from the 1890s and spells "Bread" in letters big enough to be seen by people zipping by on I-70. Originally a grain and feed shop, some remember the more modern history of Sopp & Truscott, a bakery that produced, among other things, delicious jalapeño-cheddar bread and worked on the honor system. When the bakery closed and went up for sale in 2009, Shae Whitney and Brady Becker, an enterprising young couple

who started a company called DRAM Apothecary, making drams and bitters from foraged herbs and botanicals, took over the space. They opened a tasting room—and cocktail bar—called Bread Bar. (In 2016, a group of friends—Fenberg, Casey Berry, Rob DuRay, and Sam Alvianio took over the bar when Whitney and Becker and DRAM outgrew Silver Plume.)

Bread Bar is only open on the weekends but it has nailed a niche business. The menu largely sticks to the classics and all are named after historic figures that reflect Silver Plume and Colorado's mining history. Bread Bar succeeds because it walks two lines: it's a hipster spot in a historic location where people get engaged and married *and* it meets the needs of Silver Plume's residents. For example, Bud Light isn't on the menu, but it is for a resident named Jerry, just like a specific wine is available just for Claudia. "I don't think this bar would work in Denver, or Boulder, or a bar scene with competition," Fenberg says. "It's more of a gathering place, it's an experience. We're not just a bar, we're a destination."

CLIFFORD GRIFFIN

BREAD BAR
1010 MAIN STREET, SILVER PLUME

This Sour is named after the ghost of Silver Plume. Clifford Griffin ran the Seven Thirty Mine (so titled because it opened an hour later than other area mines) on Silver Plume Mountain in the 1880s. His fiancée tragically died the day before their wedding on the East Coast and, to run from his grief, Griffin headed West to try his luck at mining. He lived in a cabin near the mine and played the violin every night as the town of Silver Plume was going to sleep. One night after playing his last song, the town heard a gunshot. Townspeople found Clifford in a grave of his own making with a note asking to bury him there. The town honored his wish and erected a large obelisk as a gravestone, which still stands today. Legend has it, if you listen carefully on a quiet summer evening, you can still hear a melancholic violin playing into the night.

GLASSWARE: Rocks glass

- **2 oz. rye whiskey**
- **½ oz. Peach Street Amaro**
- **½ oz. fresh lemon juice**
- **½ oz. Simple Syrup (see recipe on page 18)**
- **1 oz. red wine, to float**

1. Combine all of the ingredients, except for the wine, in a cocktail shaker with ice and shake vigorously.
2. Strain the cocktail into a rocks glass with fresh ice.
3. Gently pour red wine over the back of a spoon into the glass. (This allows the wine to float on top of the cocktail.)

BABY DOE TABOR

BREAD BAR
1010 MAIN STREET, SILVER PLUME

In the 1880s, Baby Doe was the second—and much younger—wife of the famous Colorado businessman and silver magnate Horace Tabor. Doe's rags-to-riches-and-back-to-rags story has made her a Colorado legend. She went from being one of the most alluring women in the mining West to a penniless eighty-one-year-old woman who froze to death in a dilapidated mining shack in Leadville. Co-owner Steve Fenberg says he and Bread Bar's staff like to think of this cocktail as one Baby Doe would sip while remembering the good ol' days.

GLASSWARE: Mason jar
GARNISH: Fresh sage leaves

- **2 oz. Jones House Vodka**
- **1½ oz. Blackberry Sage Syrup (see recipe)**
- **½ oz. fresh lemon juice**
- **½ oz. Simple Syrup (see recipe on page 18)**
- **Soda water, to top**

1. Combine all of the ingredients in a cocktail shaker with ice and shake vigorously.
2. Dirty-pour (do not strain) the cocktail into a mason jar.
3. Add additional ice, top with soda, and garnish with fresh sage leaves.

Blackberry Sage Syrup: Add equal amounts of blackberry jam and water to a saucepan and bring the mixture to a simmer. Stir occasionally until the jam is dissolved. Add a pinch of dried sage and simmer for 8 minutes. Strain and let cool. Store it in the refrigerator for up to 2 weeks.

THE BRAKEMAN

ROOTSTALK
207 NORTH MAIN STREET, BRECKENRIDGE

James Beard Award–winning chef Matt Vawter was close to naming his upscale farm-to-table restaurant in Breckenridge The Brakeman. This name references the railroad worker who had the high-pressure job of controlling the train's brakes—sort of like a chef. It's also a nod to Breckenridge's mining and railroad history. Vawter decided on Rootstalk instead because he was returning to his hometown and, thus, to his roots to open his first restaurant. The Brakeman cocktail was on the opening menu in December of 2020 and has been a favorite ever since. A variation on an Old Fashioned, this drink adds amaro for complexity and rum to draw out some of the barrel notes of the bourbon. The sarsaparilla bitters provide root beer notes.

GLASSWARE: Double rocks glass
GARNISH: Orange twist, expressed

- 1½ oz. Old Forester 100 Proof Bourbon
- ½ oz. Amaro Nonino Quintessentia
- ½ oz. Mount Gay Barbados Rum Black Barrel
- ¼ oz. Demerara Syrup (see recipe on page 18)
- 4 dashes sarsaparilla bitters
- Dash Angostura bitters

1. Combine all of the ingredients in a mixing glass with ice and stir.
2. Strain the cocktail into a double rocks glass with a large ice cube.
3. Squeeze the orange twist over the cocktail to express the oils and garnish with the twist.

NEW BOOT GOOFIN'

ROOTSTALK

207 NORTH MAIN STREET, BRECKENRIDGE

What do you get when you cross a tiki cocktail with a mezcal Spicy Margarita? In this creation from Rootstalk bartender Chad Moreau, the tropical flavors of pineapple meet the sweet heat of a Calabrian hot honey. Moreau named the drink after a bit from the mockumentary *Reno 911*.

GLASSWARE: **Collins glass**

GARNISH: **Dehydrated lime wheel, Angostura bitters**

- **1½ oz. Del Maguey Vida Clásico**
- **¾ oz. Hot Honey (see recipe)**
- **¾ oz. pineapple juice**
- **¾ oz. fresh lime juice**
- **½ oz. Giffard Caribbean Pineapple Liqueur**
- **Dash Saline Solution (see recipe on page 19)**

1. Combine all of the ingredients in a cocktail shaker tin, add ice, and shake.
2. Double-strain the cocktail into a collins glass with a large ice spear, or with ice cubes stacked one on top of another.
3. Garnish with a dehydrated lime wheel and drizzle Angostura bitters around the top, creating an ombre layer that floats.

HOT HONEY: In a high-powered blender, combine 700 grams rich honey syrup (3:1 honey to water), 200 grams Rich Simple Syrup (see recipe on page 18), and 50 grams Calabrian chile oil and blend to combine.

SHOOTING STAR SPRITZ

LOOKOUT BAR
42 RIVERFRONT LANE, AVON

At Lookout Bar, Avon's first (and only) rooftop bar, cocktail names are inspired by the area's trails and ski runs, such as Lamplighter and Shooting Star. As befits a shooting star, for this cocktail, the bar staff uses a sparkly edible dust, citrus, and bubbles in its unique presentation.

GLASSWARE: Champagne flute
GARNISH: Mint leaves

- **1 oz. Aperol**
- **1 oz. reposado tequila**
- **Barspoon lemon juice**
- **Barspoon gold luster dust**
- **3 oz. prosecco, to top**
- **1 oz. soda water, to top**

1. Shake the Aperol, tequila, lemon juice, and luster dust in a shaker tin with ice.
2. Strain the cocktail into a champagne flute and top with soda and prosecco.
3. Add one ice cube to the glass to increase the bubbles and encourage the gold to sparkle.
4. Garnish with mint leaves.

LAMPLIGHTER

LOOKOUT BAR
42 RIVERFRONT LANE, AVON

This cocktail is all about the drama. Per its name, the Lamplighter is finished with a lime husk filled with 151 rum that's set aflame. As it's burning, a bartender shakes cinnamon (it's flammable) over the drink, creating sparks. This is a playful surprise but if you choose to add the garnish, please be careful! If it's too over the top, the cocktail is still delicious without the pomp and circumstance. To swizzle, as the recipe calls for, take the top of your barspoon between both palms and quickly rub your palms against each other. This adds aeration while also diluting and mixing the drink. Of course, in a pinch, stirring rapidly with a regular spoon will do just fine.

GLASSWARE: Footed decorative glass

GARNISH: Mint; cinnamon stick, burnt at one end; lime husk

- **2 oz. spiced dark rum**
- **½ oz. orange curaçao**
- **½ oz. Pepita & Sunflower Seed Orgeat (see recipe)**
- **½ oz. fresh lime juice**
- **Dash Angostura bitters**
- **Splash 151 rum**
- **Pinch ground cinnamon**

1. Combine the dark rum, curaçao, orgeat, and lime juice in a glass.
2. Add crushed ice to the top and swizzle with a barspoon.
3. Top up with more ice and add a healthy dash of bitters to the top.
4. Place the lime husk on top of the cocktail as a small bowl and pour in the 151 rum.

5. Light the rum on fire, and carefully sprinkle ground cinnamon on top for extra sparkles.
6. When ready to drink, blow out the flame and pour the now warmed rum into the drink.
7. Garnish with mint and a smoking cinnamon stick.

PEPITA & SUNFLOWER SEED ORGEAT: In a high-speed blender, blend 8 oz. cane sugar, 8 oz. water, 2 oz. sunflower seeds, and 2 oz. pumpkin seeds together. Strain the orgeat through a fine-mesh strainer, then once more through a coffee filter. Bottle and keep the orgeat refrigerated for up to 1 month.

PUNCH AND TODDY

MOUNTAIN STANDARD
193 GORE CREEK DRIVE, VAIL

From the day Mountain Standard opened in 2012, it has been a Vail gathering spot, and bartender Keith Webber has been there almost from the beginning. In 2024, Webber won the Colorado Restaurant Association's Bartender of the Year Award and his ease behind the bar has become part of the Mountain Standard experience. This refreshingly sweet and tart spiced Hot Toddy is Webber's answer to warming up after a day on Vail's slopes. He uses spiced pear liqueur, but any flavorful fruity liqueur (such as apricot brandy) can be substituted.

GLASSWARE: Toddy glass
GARNISH: Whole cloves, pear slice

- **½ oz. Black Tea Syrup (see recipe)**
- **4 oz. hot water**
- **1½ oz. Ron Zacapa No. 23**
- **¾ oz. St. George Spiced Pear Liqueur**
- **¾ oz. fresh lemon juice**

1. Pour the syrup into a toddy glass. Cover with hot water, and stir to dissolve.
2. Add the rum, pear liqueur, and lemon juice.
3. Garnish with a couple of cloves and a pear slice.

Black Tea Syrup: Make 1 cup of strong black tea, then add 1½ cups sugar while hot. Stir to dissolve the sugar and allow the syrup to cool.

CHAMPAGNE OR DEATH

MOUNTAIN STANDARD
193 GORE CREEK DRIVE, VAIL

Bitter, sweet, and effervescent, this cocktail has become Mountain Standard's popular "back pocket cocktail" when someone requests a gin-based drink. (For those who like French 75s, this drinks similarly.) The name, Champagne or Death, comes from the protest slogan that rang out in the 1911 Champagne Riots in France.

GLASSWARE: Collins glass
GARNISH: Lemon twist

- **1½ oz. Gray Whale Gin**
- **¾ oz. St-Germain Elderflower Liqueur**
- **¾ oz. grapefruit juice**
- **¼ oz. fresh lemon juice**
- **¼ oz. Simple Syrup (see recipe on page 18)**
- **3 dashes orange bitters**
- **3 oz. prosecco, to top**

1. Combine all of the ingredients, except for the prosecco, in a shaker tin with ice.
2. Shake until cold, then top with the prosecco.
3. Strain the cocktail over fresh ice into a collins glass, and garnish with a lemon twist.

CONNIE BAKER, MARBLE DISTILLING

Walk the length of Main Street in Carbondale and you'd be hard-pressed to miss the building housing Marble Distilling. The "M" that hangs over the entrance is sharp-peaked, bold, and eye-catching. The shape recalls the West Elk Mountains that flank the town, while the bold lettering could be considered a metaphor for the path the distillery has taken.

By all accounts, Connie Baker, co-founder, CEO, and head distiller of Marble Distilling, is a pioneer. In addition to holding her own as one of the few female distillers in the industry, her mission is two-fold: she's intent on turning out gorgeous, award-winning craft spirits, and doing so in the most sustainable way possible.

Marble Distilling, which Baker opened with husband Carey Shanks in 2015, is maybe the greenest distillery on the planet. Using a water-energy thermal system that Shanks helped design, the distillery captures one hundred percent of its used hot water, and reuses the energy harvested from the distillation process to heat (or cool) the facility.

As Baker likes to joke, Marble Distilling is saving the world one bottle of vodka at a time. And it certainly doesn't hurt that the distillery crafts really, really good vodka, not to mention excellent whiskey and must-have gingercello (think limoncello but ginger).

The space, which has a front bar and a boutique inn upstairs, is designed to show off massive slabs of marble from the nearby town of the same name. In fact, the quarry where the Yule marble for the Lincoln Memorial, the Tomb of the Unknown Soldier, and the Washington Monument was mined sits just thirtyish miles to the south. Pieces of that very same marble are used, in conjunction with coconut husks, to filter Marble's spirits for a clean and pristine flavor destined to find legions of fans.

GINGERCELLO
VODKA

HAYRYED

MARBLE DISTILLING
150 MAIN STREET, CARBONDALE

The HayRyed came about as Marble Distilling built a float for Carbondale's Potato Days festival. (The annual October tradition, which will be one hundred and sixteen years old in 2025, celebrates the valley's agricultural history and the life-sustaining tuber.) For the float, Marble's crew, headed by Baker, built a mini distillery on a farm trailer, complete with a working still heated by a turkey burner. Hay bales were situated around it for riders and, as the float made its way around downtown, the still cooked moonshine.

GLASSWARE: Mason jar

GARNISH: Smoking cinnamon stick, dehydrated orange wheel

- **1½ oz. Hoovers Revenge Rye Whiskey**
- **¾ oz. Marble Distilling Gingercello**
- **¾ oz. maple syrup**
- **Apple cider, to top**

1. Combine the whiskey, liqueur, and syrup in a mason jar and stir.
2. Add ice, top with cider, and garnish with a smoking cinnamon stick and dehydrated orange wheel.

YELLOW PAGES

THE WESTERN HOTEL & SPA
210 SEVENTH AVENUE, OURAY

The Western is a historic hotel in downtown Ouray, a mountain hamlet located about fifty miles from Telluride. The hotel was originally built in 1891 but it was fully renovated in 2023. Bar manager Kelly Wood created this cocktail for fall, when the aspen leaves are turning golden and the air feels crisp. The key ingredient is the syrup, because it really highlights the calvados, while the bourbon cuts the sweetness. The syrup has big hints of coffee cake and the vanilla is a perfect enhancer to other bourbon drinks such as an Old Fashioned—that's your cue to make extra.

GLASSWARE: Nick & Nora glass
GARNISH: Dehydrated apple slice

- **1½ oz. calvados**
- **1 oz. fresh lemon juice**
- **¾ oz. Vanilla-Cinnamon Syrup (see recipe)**
- **½ oz. bourbon**

1. Chill a Nick & Nora glass. Combine all of the ingredients in a shaker tin with ice and shake until chilled.
2. Double-strain the cocktail into the chilled Nick & Nora.
3. Garnish with a dehydrated apple slice.

VANILLA-CINNAMON SYRUP: Make Rich Simple Syrup (see recipe on page 18), adding 1 tablespoon Madagascar vanilla extract and 2 cinnamon sticks as the syrup is simmering. Simmer for 30 minutes. Add the peels from 1 orange. Remove the syrup from heat and allow it to cool. Remove the orange peels but leave the cinnamon sticks in the syrup container to continue flavor development. The syrup is shelf stable and will last indefinitely without being refrigerated.

DEAD FLOWERS

THE WESTERN HOTEL & SPA
210 SEVENTH AVENUE, OURAY

When mixologist Derek Peabody was dreaming up cocktails for The Western, he mined memories of fall with his grandmother, including desserts made from her canned fruits. "Fall has always been my favorite season, especially growing up in Maine," he says.

GLASSWARE: **Coupe glass**
GARNISH: **Dehydrated lemon wheel**

- **1½ oz. gin**
- **¾ oz. crème de cacao**
- **¾ oz. fresh lemon juice**
- **¾ oz. Strawberry-Balsamic Shrub (see recipe)**

1. Chill a coupe glass. Combine all of the ingredients in a shaker tin with ice and shake until cold.
2. Double-strain the cocktail into the chilled coupe and garnish with a dehydrated lemon wheel.

STRAWBERRY-BALSAMIC SHRUB: Add 1½ cups hulled and sliced strawberries and 1 cup unrefined cane sugar to a large, airtight bowl or container. Muddle together and let the mixture sit for 30 minutes. Add ¼ cup balsamic vinegar and ¾ cup raw apple cider vinegar. Close the container and refrigerate it, undisturbed, for 48 hours. Strain, and reserve the strawberries for another use, like a charcuterie board.

LANDO

THE WESTERN HOTEL & SPA
210 SEVENTH AVENUE, OURAY

If you live in Colorado (or visit the state during harvest season) you know the magic of a Palisade peach. "The town of Palisade is known for its peaches and people come from all over every year to get ahold of them," mixologist Eric Nunn says. "The fruit has the perfect sweetness, and we like to make a syrup out of it to make various drinks over the season." In this cocktail, the smokiness of the mezcal, paired with the bitterness of Campari and the sweetness of the peaches, tastes of summer. Also try the syrup in a Peach Bourbon Smash, vodka drinks, or nonalcoholic Spritzes.

GLASSWARE: Coupe glass
GARNISH: Lemon twist

- **1½ oz. mezcal**
- **1 oz. fresh lemon juice**
- **¾ oz. Campari**
- **½ oz. Peach Syrup (see recipe)**

1. Chill a coupe glass. Combine all of the ingredients in a cocktail shaker with ice and shake until cold.
2. Double-strain the cocktail into the chilled coupe and garnish with a lemon twist.

Peach Syrup: Make Rich Simple Syrup (see recipe on page 18) and allow it to cool. Weigh peaches, as needed, peeled, pitted, and cubed, and measure equal parts of the syrup you just made to the weight of the peaches. Combine them in a saucepan over medium-low heat and simmer for at least 60 minutes. Once the peaches have started to break down, stir the syrup and taste for flavor. Once you reach a rich peach flavor, turn off the heat and let the mixture cool.

STEVE FOSTER, NEW SHERIDAN HOTEL

Almost despite itself, Telluride has a signature cocktail. The man credited with the drink—the Flatliner—laughs at the distinction just as much as he shrugs off the cocktail itself. "It tastes like dessert, but to each his own. I mean, a lot of people like pink Cadillacs and gold stuff on their furniture," says Steve Foster, a local bartender, who has spent the better part of two decades working at the New Sheridan Hotel on Telluride's main drag.

As the story goes, the cocktail, a shaken blend of vodka, Baileys, Kahlúa, and espresso (which is essentially a Mudslide), came to town with a New Zealand wedding party in 1995 or 1996. "I was working at the Peak's Resort and I was the bartender on duty when the wedding party requested a special cocktail called 'the Flatliner.'" It was shaken, served in a cordial glass, and each espresso shot had to be pulled manually. In Foster's view, the Flatliner was "a pain in the butt. I spent the night pulling a million espresso shots."

For whatever reason, the Flatliner took on a life of its own. The staff the night of the wedding liked the cocktail and began requesting it when Foster was behind the bar at the New Sheridan. "It started spreading," he says. "People would see them come out to a table and they'd want to order them too. It was like a little fire that kept on growing." The cocktail is so popular that in the bar's speedwells, the number-one spots—usually reserved for vodka, gin, and rum—are occupied by vodka, Baileys, and Kahlúa.

At first, other restaurants would send guests requesting Flatliners to the New Sheridan—until they wised up and started adding the drink to their menus. Local bartenders began to reach out to Foster, asking if they could modify the cocktail, to which he shrugged and said to have at it. "A lot of people think I'm the inventor of it," he says. "I was just the conduit. I just happened to be working that night."

Over time, the cocktail has gained such notoriety that a local competition—The Flatliner Face/Off—sprang up in October of 2024. And what does Foster have to say about that? "I really didn't want anything to do with it. My favorite cocktail is a finger of bourbon."

THE FLATLINER

NEW SHERIDAN HOTEL
231 WEST COLORADO AVENUE, TELLURIDE

The original recipe is below, but note that, over time, bartender Steve Foster has slightly modified the measurements. "This is my version: It's equal parts Baileys, Kahlúa, and espresso, plus a heavy pour (at least 2 ounces) of vodka to cut the sweetness," he says.

GLASSWARE: Cordial glass

- **1 oz. vodka**
- **1 oz. Baileys Original Irish Cream**
- **1 oz. Kahlúa**
- **1 shot espresso**

1. Combine all of the ingredients in a cocktail shaker with ice and shake.
2. Strain the cocktail into a cordial glass.

RIPPERS REPOSE

DUNTON HOT SPRINGS
8532 ROAD 38, RICO

In 2001, Dunton Hot Springs, an 1880s mining town about thirty miles from Telluride, was recast as a luxury, all-inclusive resort. There, Rippers Repose has become the ideal cocktail to celebrate a day spent in the great outdoors. Anchored by whiskey and botanical notes, the cocktail is usually enjoyed by guests on the saloon's deck taking in views of the San Juan Mountains, or at the bar while admiring Butch Cassidy's hand-carved moniker. Dunton prides itself on supporting local purveyors, and the Rippers Repose showcases The Decc, a distinctive whiskey, citrus, and clove liqueur by Colorado Springs–based 291 Distillery.

GLASSWARE: Rocks glass
GARNISH: Orange twist

- **1½ oz. The Decc Citrus Clove Liqueur**
- **1 oz. cranberry juice**
- **¼ oz. fresh lemon juice**
- **Soda water, to top**

1. Fill a rocks glass with ice.
2. Pour in The Decc, cranberry juice, and lemon juice, then top with soda water. Stir gently to combine.
3. Garnish with an orange twist.

FENNEL & ROSEMARY RICKEY

MAMBO
521 LINCOLN AVENUE, STEAMBOAT SPRINGS

Chef Hannah Hopkins' combined loves for St. George Terroir Gin and living in the mountains inspired this cocktail. "I wanted to complement this California gin with my favorite Italian flavors like fennel and rosemary," she says. "Sipping on this drink transports you to the forest with its notes of pine, licorice, and fresh lime."

GLASSWARE: Collins glass
GARNISH: Black pepper, rosemary sprig

- **1½ oz. St. George Terroir Gin**
- **1 oz. Don Ciccio & Figli Finocchietto**
- **1 oz. Rosemary Syrup (see recipe)**
- **¾ oz. fresh lemon juice**
- **¾ oz. fresh lime juice**

1. Combine all of the ingredients in a cocktail shaker with ice and shake.
2. Strain the cocktail over ice into a collins glass.
3. Top with soda and more ice if needed, and garnish with black pepper and a sprig of rosemary.

ROSEMARY SYRUP: Make Simple Syrup (see recipe on page 18), adding 4 sprigs of rosemary to the cooling syrup. Steep overnight, strain, and store the syrup in the refrigerator.

TIPSY CARROT

BÉSAME
818 LINCOLN AVENUE, STEAMBOAT SPRINGS

When Steamboat Springs chef Hannah Hopkins opened Bésame in 2018, the New York City transplant wanted a Margarita that fit the Latin-inspired concept: bright, flavorful, spicy, and ahead of its time. "When I started playing with fresh-pressed carrot juice, spicy habanero, and tequila, I knew I was on to something," she says. In the time since, the sweet, spicy, sour, savory, and salty combo has not only become Bésame's bestselling cocktail, but also a Steamboat favorite.

GLASSWARE: **Margarita glass**
GARNISH: **Fresno chile, cilantro sprig**

- **Smoked salt, for the rim**
- **1½ oz. Suerte Blanco Tequila**
- **1½ oz. carrot juice**
- **1 oz. fresh lime juice**
- **¾ oz. Chile Simple Syrup (see recipe)**
- **4 drops habanero bitters**

1. Wet the rim of a margarita glass with lime juice then dip the glass in smoked salt to give the glass a rim.
2. Combine the remaining ingredients in a cocktail shaker with ice and shake.
3. Strain the cocktail into the rimmed glass.
4. Garnish with a Fresno chile and cilantro sprig.

Chile Simple Syrup: Cut 1 Fresno chile and 1 jalapeño pepper in half, remove the seeds, and place the chiles in a heatproof bowl. Add 2 cups sugar and top with 2 cups boiling hot water. Stir to dissolve the sugar and let the syrup cool overnight. Store in the refrigerator for up to 2 weeks.

HARVEST MOON (NA)

YAMPA VALLEY KITCHEN
207 NINTH STREET, STEAMBOAT SPRINGS

The Harvest Moon, Yampa Valley Kitchen's nonalcoholic Old Fashioned, grew out of a toasted corn tea that bartender Liberty Adams makes. "Toasting the corn husk unlocks all of the flavors in the husk without it tasting like food," he says. Combined with chamomile, used bourbon chips, honey, vanilla, and lemon peel, Adams knew the brew had real potential. "The complementary nature of corn and bourbon drove me to make it into a nonalcoholic Old Fashioned over a big rock."

GLASSWARE: Rocks glass

GARNISH: Dried chamomile flower, lemon peel

- **2 oz. Roasted Corn Tea (see recipe)**
- **½ oz. Chamomile Husk Honey Syrup (see recipe)**
- **Dash vanilla extract**
- **Dash lemon extract**

1. Combine all of the ingredients in a rocks glass with a big ice cube and stir until chilled.
2. Garnish with a dried chamomile flower and lemon peel.

ROASTED CORN TEA: Combine 1 cup boiling hot water and ¼ cup roasted corn in a heatproof bowl. Steep for 15 minutes, then strain and allow the tea to cool.

Chamomile Husk Honey Syrup: Combine 1 cup local honey, 1 cup boiling hot water, 1 tablespoon dried chamomile, and the husk of 1 ear of corn in a heatproof bowl. Steep for 15 minutes, strain, and store in the refrigerator for up to 2 weeks.

HAIKU SPRITZ

YAMPA VALLEY KITCHEN
207 NINTH STREET, STEAMBOAT SPRINGS

"The Haiku came about from a Spritz I made on the fly for a guest featuring Chareau [an aloe liqueur made in California]," says bartender Liberty Adams. "Chareau is awesome, but it's better at supporting flavors rather than being the star of the show." In thinking about complementary flavors, Adams turned to melon, though he was wary of using actual melon because he worried the water content would dilute the flavor. He landed on Midori Melon Liqueur and added cardamom for oomph to a drink that felt delicate.

GLASSWARE: Wineglass

GARNISH: Cucumber ribbon, lemon half-moon

- **3 oz. prosecco, divided**
- **¾ oz. Midori Melon Liqueur**
- **¾ oz. Chareau**
- **¾ oz. lemon vodka**
- **¾ oz. fresh lemon juice**
- **Dash Cardamom Extract (see recipe)**

1. Pour 2 oz. prosecco into a wineglass.
2. Place a cucumber ribbon in a cocktail shaker with ice.
3. Add the remaining ingredients, except for the remaining prosecco, to the shaker and shake.
4. Pour the cocktail into the wineglass and top with the remaining prosecco.
5. Garnish with half of a lemon wheel.

CARDAMOM EXTRACT: Combine 1 tablespoon whole cardamom pods, crushed, and 3 oz. vodka in an airtight container and let the infusion sit for 24 hours. Strain and store for up to 1 month.

METANOIA

THE BOOKCASE AND BARBER
601 EAST SECOND AVENUE, SUITE B, DURANGO

Durango's best secret is a barbershop with a hidden cocktail bar. Go in for a haircut, figure out the password, and pass through the door for a speakeasy experience. The Metanoia, which was one of the very first cocktails from the Winter 2015 menu, isn't on The Bookcase and Barber's printed menu anymore, but if you know to ask, Beau Black, who owns the place with his wife, Jenna, will still make it for you. The cocktail blends a beautiful Earl Grey–lavender gin with a locally distilled vodka from Loveland, and finishes it with a smooth mouthfeel contributed by foamed egg whites.

GLASSWARE: **Large coupe glass**

GARNISH: **2 dashes Angostura bitters swirled with a skewer**

- **¾ oz. egg whites**
- **¾ oz. fresh lemon juice**
- **1½ oz. Earl Grey-Lavender Gin (see recipe)**
- **¾ oz. Carpano Bianco**
- **¾ oz. grenadine**
- **¼ oz. Honey Syrup (see recipe on page 18)**

1. Combine the egg whites and lemon juice in a cocktail shaker tin with the spring from a Hawthorne strainer and dry-shake (without ice).
2. Add the remaining ingredients and a few ice cubes and shake again, until the metal is too cold to hold.
3. Strain the cocktail into a large coupe. There should be ½ inch of white foam once it separates. Garnish with bitters on top of the foam and swirl with a skewer.

Earl Grey–Lavender Gin: Add 1 oz. dried Earl Grey-lavender tea to 1 liter Spring44 Gin. Let the tea infuse the gin for 4 hours at room temperature. Strain and store.

CELTIC KANTHAROS

THE BOOKCASE AND BARBER
601 EAST SECOND AVENUE, SUITE B, DURANGO

For years, Beau Black worked in kitchens across Colorado, and he always looked forward to the mountain harvest of late-summer, early-fall chanterelles. Infusing culinary flavors—such as these treasured mushrooms—into cocktails is an experience Black is proud to share. Note that there really is no substitute for fresh chanterelles. If you can't find them fresh, wait until you can get them before making this cocktail. To dry your own chanterelles, dehydrate them in a food dehydrator at 130°F for 24 hours.

GLASSWARE: Small coupe glass
GARNISH: Dried chanterelle with clothespin

- **2 oz. Brown Butter–Washed Irish Whiskey (see recipe)**
- **½ oz. Osborne Medium Sherry**
- **¼ oz. honey**
- **Dash black walnut bitters**
- **3 drops Saline Solution (see recipe on page 19)**

1. Combine all of the ingredients in a mixing glass with ice and stir.
2. Strain the cocktail into a small coupe and garnish with a dried chanterelle affixed with a clothespin.

Brown Butter–Washed Irish Whiskey: In a pan over medium heat, sauté 1 cup fresh chanterelles and a sprig of thyme in 1 pound brown butter. Remove the mixture from heat and allow it to cool. In a large container, combine the mixture and 1 liter Irish whiskey. Shake every hour for 3 hours. Place the whiskey in the freezer overnight, then strain through a coffee filter. Reserve the butter, chanterelles, and thyme for your next meal.

THE WESTERN SLOPE

VALLEY CURSE

MARG FOR STEVIE

WHERE IS MY MIND

KICK PUSH

TACOPARTY MARGARITA

At its most basic, "the Western Slope" refers to anything west of the Continental Divide. But like most colloquialisms, it has many definitions. If you haven't noticed already, the Continental Divide features heavily in Colorado-speak. The jagged spine of 11,000-foot mountains not only divides the state in two (although not quite equally); it's also a landmark used to denote ways of life: city living (east), and mountain living and farming (west). While not entirely accurate, because there's certainly city living in the west and farming in the east, most residents still glom on to this way of thinking. In addition to the natural dividing line, the Eisenhower-Johnson Memorial Tunnel, which travels a mile underneath the Continental Divide, is also code for going east or west.

When you're in Denver and you travel west, you're headed to the mountains. And when you continue west, you land in the state's fruit belt. Here, thousands of acres are devoted to meandering grapevines and plush apple, peach, apricot, plum, and cherry orchards. This fruit basket is what the Western Slope is known for, and there are days during harvest season where the air is perfumed by the intoxicating scent of stone fruit. Without the continuous bustle of a large city, life feels slower here and more tied to the natural rhythms of the land and seasons.

VALLEY CURSE

MELROSE SPIRIT CO.
337 COLORADO AVENUE, GRAND JUNCTION

Melrose Spirit Co. is a cozy twenty-two-seat bar located inside the historic Hotel Melrose in Grand Junction. The circa 1908 hotel, which ran continuously until 2021, underwent a complete remodel in October 2023. The lobby bar also got the same polished treatment and offers "a unique slice of paradise in the high desert," says Melrose Spirit Co. owner Gavin Bistodeau. The menu is largely rooted in classic cocktails, but many of the offerings, such as this one, have a refreshing tropical twist.

GLASSWARE: Double rocks glass
GARNISH: Half pineapple wheel

- **¾ oz. mezcal**
- **¾ oz. blanc vermouth**
- **½ oz. Cocchi Americano**
- **¼ oz. Luxardo Bitter Bianco**
- **¼ oz. Giffard Caribbean Pineapple Liqueur**

1. Combine all of the ingredients in a double rocks glass.
2. Add a large ice cube and stir for 5 to 10 seconds.
3. Garnish with half of a pineapple wheel.

MARG FOR STEVIE

MELROSE SPIRIT CO.
337 COLORADO AVENUE, GRAND JUNCTION

In a town known for its mountain-biking trails and vibrant craft-beer culture, owner Gavin Bistodeau says that Melrose Spirit Co. is proud to offer something a little different. The bar specializes in agave spirits and rum, which it utilizes in a majority of the menu's cocktails. Marg for Stevie recalls the Margarita but with a tropical note. It's perfect for sipping under the bar's blazing "This Must Be the Place" neon sign.

GLASSWARE: Tiki mug
GARNISH: Pineapple fronds, cucumber wheels sprinkled with Tajín

- **1½ oz. blanco tequila**
- **¾ oz. fresh lime juice**
- **¾ oz. pineapple juice**
- **½ oz. cucumber vodka**
- **½ oz. passion fruit syrup**
- **¼ oz. Spiced Honey Syrup (see recipe)**
- **¼ oz. Ancho Reyes Original Ancho Chile Liqueur**

1. Combine all of the ingredients in a cocktail shaker tin with pebble ice and shake.
2. Pour the cocktail into a tiki mug and top with fresh ice.
3. Garnish with pineapple fronds and cucumber wheels sprinkled with Tajín.

Spiced Honey Syrup: In a saucepan, combine 2 cups honey, 1 cup water, 2 cinnamon sticks, and 2 allspice berries and cook on medium heat for 15 minutes without boiling. Remove from heat and allow the syrup to infuse for 2 hours. Strain and refrigerate for up to 1 month.

JOSH NIERNBERG, BIN 707 FOODBAR AND TACOPARTY

In many ways, Grand Junction is Colorado's red-headed stepchild. Despite being the biggest metropolis on the Western Slope and sitting at the center of the state's wine country, fruit orchards, and many farms and ranches, many drivers don't even deem GJ stop-worthy when cruising by on I-70. That is a shame because the small city/big town has a ton to offer in the way of charm, personality, and two insanely creative restaurants.

Getting folks to pull off at the Grand Junction exit has been James Beard–nominated chef Josh Niernberg's mission the last fifteen years. He is a tireless champion of the area's agricultural riches, all of which show up in the creative dishes and cocktails at his restaurants Bin 707 Foodbar and Tacoparty.

Niernberg opened Bin 707 in 2011, and he did so with a hyperlocal focus. These days, that might sound trite as many chefs profess to have that same mission. But the rare few take it as seriously as Niernberg. He dug in so deep that he refused to use citrus on his menus because lemons, limes, oranges, and grapefruit don't grow in Colorado or neighboring states.

In 2017, when Niernberg opened Tacoparty, a taco shop also rooted in ingredients grown, sourced, and made within the heart of Colorado's Grand Valley, his ban on citrus proved exponentially more difficult. "It's hard to do Margaritas without citrus," he says. But he put his mind to it, figured out sourcing, and tried his very best to stay in the local lane. "We used verjus [the very tart pressed juice of unripened grapes] for a long time, but we don't have a great verjus source anymore," Niernberg says. "We were also using Big B's cider vinegar. It was made with really local fruit and we could get the acid we needed but then they stopped making it."

Ultimately, the unreliable nature of sourcing and the varying degrees of quality products forced his hand: Niernberg expanded Bin 707 and Tacoparty's focus to include regional ingredients. "And by regional, I mean expanding to the West Coast," he says. Now he leans on fresh citrus products from the West Coast to get the pop and zip he's looking for on the plate and in the glass. "We use Mommenpop [a line of California-based citrus apéritifs] and we cycle through their orange and grapefruit aperitifs," he says.

Niernberg calls his cooking style "New West," which is to say it's focused on local ingredients and techniques but often has a global perspective. The cocktails coming out of Bin 707 and Tacoparty do the same. Niernberg's insane creativity—just check out the mushroom-leaning Old Fashioned Where Is My Mind cocktail—has nabbed him multiple James Beard nominations and too many local awards to count. "It's totally beyond, but it's also achievable," he says of the cocktail, but Niernberg could just as easily be speaking about the importance of pushing the boundaries.

WHERE IS MY MIND

BIN 707 FOODBAR
400 MAIN STREET, GRAND JUNCTION

On paper, this cocktail is about as weird as it gets. It's got dashi-washed whiskey, huitlacoche bitters, and a candied enoki mushroom garnish. In the glass it should be weird too, but instead each sip is smooth, balanced, and totally divine. The name, Where Is My Mind, is a Pixies song, and it underscores chef-owner Josh Niernberg's dedication to thinking outside of the box when working with local ingredients and wasting as little as possible. Corn is a Colorado crop and huitlacoche is an edible fungus that grows on corn and has distinct sweet and earthy flavors that lend depth to bitters. The spent mushrooms used in many of Bin 707's stocks are repurposed when they are quickly sauteed in butter before lending their flavor to whiskey. The cocktail was a group effort between Niernberg, general manager Jeremy Arthur, and bar manager Shaleen Walz.

GLASSWARE: Rocks glass

GARNISH: Candied Enoki Mushroom (see recipe)

- **2 oz. Dashi Butter–Washed Bourbon (see recipe)**
- **¼ oz. Rich Demerara Syrup (see recipe on page 18)**
- **¼ oz. Huitlacoche Bitters (see recipe)**

1. Combine all of the ingredients in a mixing glass with ice and stir, until the mixture reaches 29°F.
2. Strain the cocktail over a large, clear ice cube into a rocks glass.
3. Garnish with Candied Enoki Mushroom.

Dashi Butter-Washed Bourbon: Melt ½ pound unsalted butter in a pan over medium-low heat. Add 250 grams dashi solids (shiitake mushrooms and kombu cooked together with water into a broth and then strained) and simmer over low heat for 20 minutes, being careful not to brown the butter. Strain the solids out of the melted butter. In a large glass container, mix the melted butter with 1 (750 ml) bottle of Elijah Craig Small Batch, stirring vigorously. Let the wash infuse overnight in the freezer. Strain the bourbon through a cheesecloth or a coffee filter and rebottle.

Huitlacoche Bitters: In a glass jar, combine 200 grams Elijah Craig Small Batch Bourbon, 5 grams dehydrated huitlacoche, and 2.5 grams Angostura bitters and cover. Infuse for 72 hours, shaking periodically. Fine-strain and bottle the bitters.

Candied Enoki Mushroom: Combine 1,200 grams granulated sugar and 600 grams water in a saucepan over high heat and bring the mixture to a boil. Immediately reduce the heat to a low simmer. Submerge 1 package of enoki mushrooms as one clump, simmering until they begin to soften. Turn off the heat and remove the enoki from the pan. Separate the mushroom clump into two to three stalk segments and arrange them in a single layer on a dehydrator sheet, keeping the segments from touching. Dehydrate at 105°F for 24 hours. Remove them from the dehydrator and store them in a cool, dry place.

KICK PUSH

BIN 707 FOODBAR
400 MAIN STREET, GRAND JUNCTION

When Bin 707 first opened in 2011, the restaurant had a Spicy Margarita on the menu. Fourteen years and many menu iterations later, that drink is still requested—and its concept still tinkered with. "The idea of a bright, green, somewhat spicy sauce to emulate the flavor profile of a Spicy Margarita but substituting the sorrel for tart and bitter balance rather than using lime, has proven to be the perfect technique for what has become our most popular drink on our menu," chef-owner Josh Niernberg says. This cocktail is a true culmination of his "New West" flavor profile and ethos. The Kick Push cocktail is named after a song by Lupe Fiasco, which is about skateboarding—one of Niernberg's favorite hobbies. Note: This recipe requires a juicer.

GLASSWARE: Rocks glass

- **1½ oz. Salsa Verde (see recipe)**
- **1 oz. Arette Blanco Tequila**
- **½ oz. Espina Negra Mezcal Espadín**
- **½ oz. Honey Syrup (see recipe on page 18)**
- **½ oz. Super Lime Juice (see recipe on page 275)**

1. Combine all of the ingredients and ice in a cocktail shaker and shake vigorously, until the shaker is frosty.
2. Strain the cocktail over a large, clear ice cube into a rocks glass.

Salsa Verde: First, consider wearing gloves while handling the chiles. Combine 1 kilogram cucumber juice; 50 to 75 grams fresh serrano pepper juice, to taste; 200 grams parsley juice; 400 grams sorrel juice; 10 grams gastrique (vinegar and sugar syrup); 15 grams honey; 10 grams salt; and 5 grams xanthan gum in a blender. Blend on high for 60 seconds, or until well incorporated.

TACOPARTY MARGARITA

TACOPARTY
125 S. FIFTH STREET, GRAND JUNCTION

Tacoparty, a fantastic taco shop in Grand Junction, is the sister restaurant to Josh Niernberg's Bin 707. And just like Bin, Tacoparty is designed to be creative and as local as possible. "Our ethos is regionally sourced cuisine so our entire menu explores how to decrease our reliance on not very sustainable (to us) citrus fruit," Niernberg explains. "One of the big contributors allowing us to do so is the use of verjus rather than relying solely on citrus." For the house Marg, the crew makes a super lime juice (the citrus juice and peels are steeped with citric acid, malic acid, and water, which drastically increases their yields) and then balances the lime with a late-harvest verjus.

GLASSWARE: Pint glass
GARNISH: Edible flowers

- **1½ oz. Arette Blanco Tequila**
- **½ oz. Horizon Late Harvest Verjus**
- **½ oz. Mommenpop Ruby Grapefruit**
- **1 oz. Super Lime Juice (see recipe)**
- **¼ oz. Rich Simple Syrup (see recipe on page 18)**
- **Salt, for the rim**

1. Combine all of the ingredients, except for the salt, with ice in a cocktail shaker and shake vigorously, until the cocktail shaker becomes frosty.
2. Salt the rim of a pint glass and add fresh ice.
3. Strain the cocktail into the rimmed glass.

Super Lime Juice: Peel limes, as needed, with a vegetable peeler, reserving the limes, and reserving and weighing the peels. Add powdered acids to the peels in the following proportions by weight: lime peels : citric acid : malic acid = 100 : 66 : 34. Stir the acid powders and peels together and let the mixture sit for at least 30 minutes. Juice the limes and set aside the juice. Add 16.67 times the weight of lime peels in water to the peels-and-acids mixture. Transfer the mixture to a blender and blend on high for 60 seconds. Combine the blended mixture with the reserved lime juice, and strain the juice through a nut milk bag.

Photo Credits

Page 25 Chad Larson; pages 30, 33, 137 Shawn Campbell; pages 35, 36–37, 39, 41, 43, 44, 47, 67, 69, 70–71, 73, 75, 76, 79, 81, 82, 85, 113, 115, 165, 166, 207 , 209, 210, 222 Connor Stehr; pages 48, 179 Casey Wilson; page 51 Taylor Fremling; pages 53, 55, 57, 59, 92, 93, 95, 97, 99, 101, 102, 105, 111, 161 Jeff Fierberg; pages 63, 65 Harrison Warters; page 86 Sash Levitov Photography; pages 89, 90 Holden Kudla; pages 107, 109 Sigri Strand; pages 120, 123 Chelsea Chorpenning; pages 125, 127 Kate Rose; page 129 Josh Brasted; page 133 Shawn Campbell; page 134 Luke Gottlieb; pages 140, 143, 145 Kelly Calvillo; pages 157, 159 Eric Bronson; page 162 Lucy Beaugard; page 170 Jen Judge; page 177 From The Hip Photo; page 189 Lucas Herbert; pages 193, 195, 197 Micah Groenevelt; page 198 Abby Dyke; pages 201, 204 Joe Newton; page 203 Kelly Lemon; page 213 Liam Doran; page 218 Cait Shaffer; pages 220, 221 Jeremy McGrew; page 225 Lauren DeFilippo; pages 232, 235 Sara Rebeka; pages 241, 242, 245 Kelly Wood; page 251 Crystal Brindle; pages 253, 255 Danielle Zimmerer; pages 257, 259 Jenna Black; page 269 Kaylan Robinson; pages 271, 273 Adam Evarts/Bin 707.

Page 9 courtesy of the Library of Congress.

Pages 1, 3, 4–5, 6, 20–21, 146–147, 169, 180–181, 260–261, used under official license from Shutterstock.com.

All other photos courtesy of their respective bars or profile subjects.

Acknowledgments

Amanda M. Faison would like to thank her husband, Heath Kirschner, for shaking and stirring up cocktails anytime she asks; Christine Bayles Kortsch for her keen eye; and all the bartenders, bar owners, and PR gurus who dealt with her onslaught of requests and questions. A bonus shout-out to all the baristas and breakfast burrito makers who kept her caffeinated and fed while writing this book.

About the Author

Amanda M. Faison has been covering food and beverage in Colorado and the West for nearly 25 years. She was the food editor of *5280*, Denver's city magazine, for a dozen years and has freelanced for publications ranging from *Food & Wine* to *Outside Magazin*e. She's edited multiple cookbooks and has sat on both the James Beard Foundation's Cookbook Awards Committee and the Restaurant & Chef Committee. Her favorite cocktails are the Vieux Carré and one she calls the Author's Note, an Italicus spritz with extra olives and plenty of olive brine.

MEASUREMENT CONVERSIONS

	1 dash		0.625 ml
	4 dashes		2.5 ml
	1 teaspoon		5 ml
¼ oz.			7.5 ml
⅓ oz.	2 teaspoons		10 ml
½ oz.	3 teaspoons	1 tablespoon	15 ml
⅔ oz.	4 teaspoons		20 ml
¾ oz.			22.5 ml
17/20 oz.			25 ml
1 oz.		2 tablespoons	30 ml
1½ oz.		3 tablespoons	45 ml
1¾ oz.			52.5 ml
2 oz.	4 tablespoons	¼ cup	60 ml
8 oz.		1 cup	250 ml
16 oz.	1 pint	2 cups	500 ml
24 oz.		3 cups	750 ml
32 oz.	1 quart	4 cups	1 liter (1,000 ml)

Index

–About Cider Mill Press Book Publishers–

Good ideas ripen with time. From seed to harvest, Cider Mill Press brings fine reading, information, and entertainment together between the covers of its creatively crafted books. Our Cider Mill bears fruit twice a year, publishing a new crop of titles each spring and fall.

"Where Good Books Are Ready for Press"
501 Nelson Place
Nashville, Tennessee 37214
cidermillpress.com

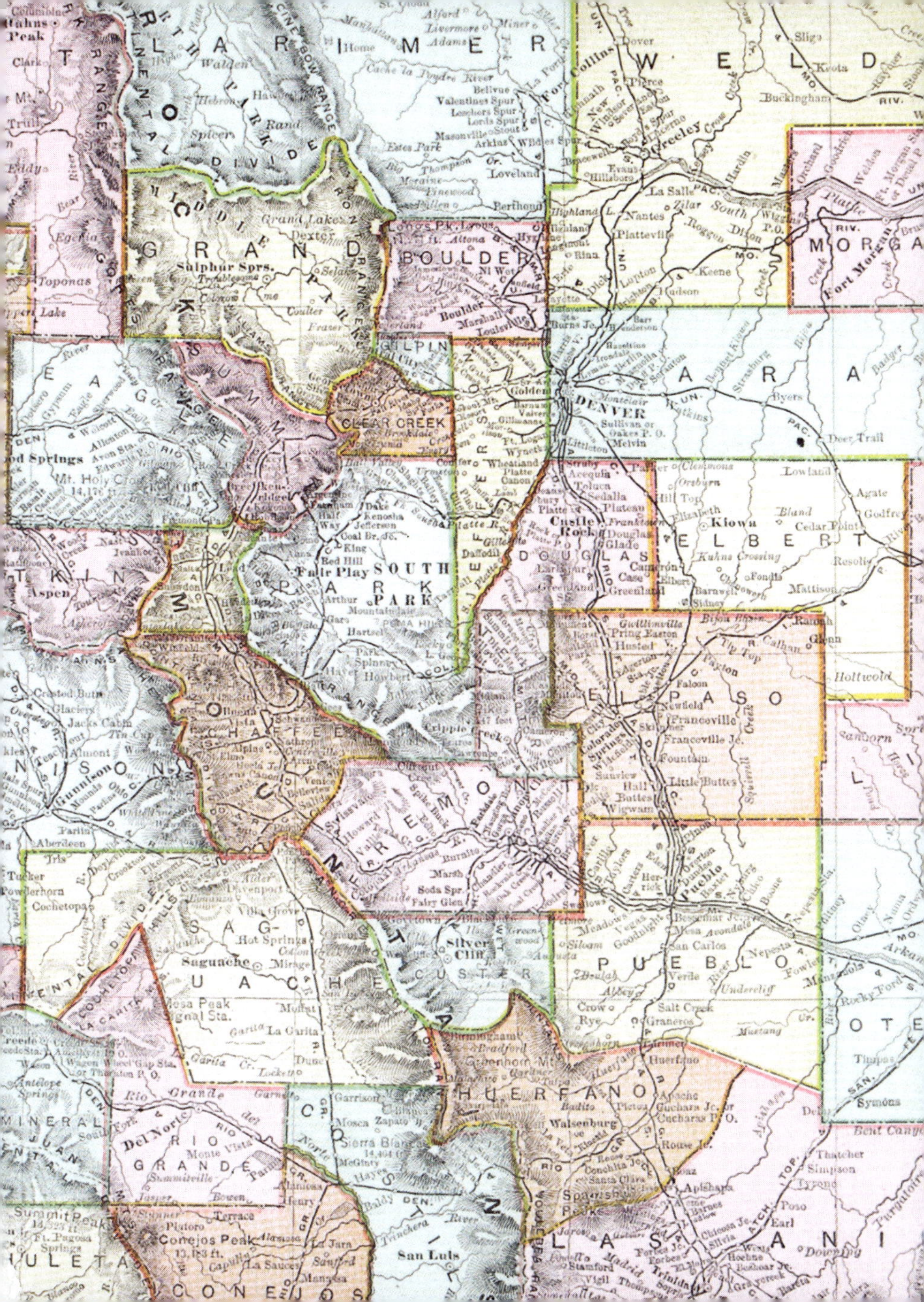

L A R I M E R
W E L D
GRAND
BOULDER
MORGAN
Fort Collins
Greeley
Loveland
Berthoud
Fort Morgan
Grand Lake
Sulphur Sprs.
Boulder
GILPIN
CLEAR CREEK
Golden
DENVER
Littleton
Deer Trail
Byers
Aspen
Fair Play
SOUTH PARK
Castle Rock
DOUGLAS
ELBERT
Kiowa
EL PASO
Colorado Springs
Cripple Creek
CHAFFEE
Gunnison
FREMONT
Pueblo
PUEBLO
Silver Cliff
CUSTER
SAGUACHE
Saguache
Villa Grove
HUERFANO
Walsenburg
Del Norte
RIO GRANDE
Monte Vista
MINERAL
COSTILLA
San Luis
CONEJOS
Conejos Peak
Trinidad
Rocky Ford
Aberdeen
Powderhorn
Cochetopa
La Garita
Moffat
Hot Springs
Mt. Holy Cross
Crested Butte
Spanish Peaks
Sierra Blanca

R O U T T
Mt. Weltha
Bear Mt.
Escalante
ESCALANTE HILLS
Maybell
Lily
Hamilton
Craig
Hayden
Eddy
Axial
DANFORTH HILLS
WILLIAMS RIVER
Walden
Hebron
Rand
Spicer
CONTINENTAL DIVIDE
M I D D L E
G R A N D
Grand Lakes
Dexter
Sulphur Sprs.
Coulter
Fraser
Angora
Rangely
R I O B L A N C O
White River
Meeker
Marvines Lakes
Toponas
Trappers Lake
WHITE RIVER PLATEAU
E A G L E
CATHEDRAL BLUFFS
Austin
Glenwood Springs
Mt. Holy Cross 14,176 ft.
Highmore
G A R F I E L D
Parachute
BATTLEMENT MESA
De Beque
Collbran
Vega
Eagalite
Cabeza
Snipes
Tunnel
Aspen
P I T K I N
Ivanhoe
Fair Play
Red Hill
Arthur
Grand Junction
Unaweep
GRAND MESA
Whitewater
Kahnah
Deer Run
D E L T A
Eckert
Paonia
Hotchkiss
Delta
Pittsburg
Anthracite
Irwin
Crested Butte
Gothic
Ruby
Baldwin
Jacks Cabin
Castleton
Hinkles
Almont
Tin Cup
WEST ELK MTS.
G U N N I S O N
Gunnison
Parlin
Aberdeen
Iola
C H A F F E E
Nathrop
Alpine
St. Elmo
Salida
UNCOMPAHGRE VALLEY
Colorow
Menoken
Montrose
Uncompahgre
M O N T R O S E
Cimarron
Marion
Grabiola
Tucker
Powderhorn
Cochetopa
Allen
Gateview
Eldredge
Colona
Naturita
Shenandoah
Dallas
Ridgway
Youman
Villa Grove
Hot Springs
Saguache
Mirage
S A G U A C H E
O U R A Y
Ouray
Lake City
Placerville
S A N M I G U E L
Fall Creek
San Miguel
Telluride
Ophir
Cedar
LONE MESA
Silverton
Creede
Wagon Wheel Gap Sta.
Antelope Springs
Mesa Peak Signal Sta.
La Garita
Moffat
D O L O R E S
Rico
H I N S D A L E
M I N E R A L
Del Norte
Monte Vista
R I O G R A N D E
Summitville
Mosca
M O N T E Z U M A
L A P L A T A
Dolores
Pagosa